EARLY BRITISH
STEAM

EARLY BRITISH STEAM

Title page: GNR No. 1, built at
Doncaster in 1870, seen in steam
at Rothley.

Right: An early Liverpool &
Manchester Railway train passes
through Olive Mount Cutting while
the walls are being widened. From an
Ackermann print of 1833.

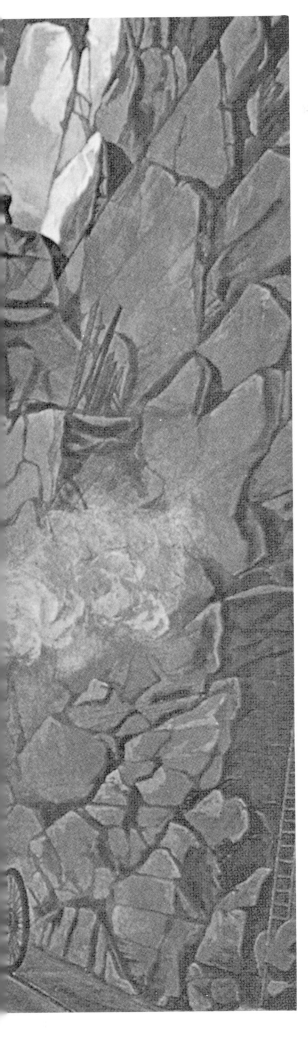

CONTENTS

RAILWAYS ARE BORN

left:
Steam was first used to power fixed or stationary engines mainly to pump water in mines or collieries. Although this print shows the two engines used to haul trains from Euston to Camden Town on the London & Birmingham Railway, their purpose, to move the steel ropes, was not new in the 1830s.

It is just a century and a half since the first railways, built specifically for carrying passengers and planned from the start for operation by steam locomotives, were opened to lay the foundations of the British railway system that we know today. The Liverpool & Manchester, and the Canterbury & Whitstable railways, both opened in 1830, confirmed the successful combination of the steam locomotive with the iron rail as a potent new form of transport which, within a decade, began to spread its tentacles not only across Britain but also into other parts of the world. Yet railways and steam power had originally developed independently and it was not until the early nineteenth century that the first real moves were made to bring them together.

The origin of the railway in the form of a guidance system for carts and wagons is lost in the mists of history. The Romans were known to have dug ruts in mountain roads to prevent wheeled vehicles from straying too close to the edge of the precipice. By the fifteenth century mines in central Europe had timber baulks to provide a smooth route over rough ground for the hand barrows of the miners; the system was later improved to include a guide pin running between baulks of timber to prevent the barrow wheels from running off the edges of the planks. Where larger horse-drawn wagons were used, a raised timber edge rail stopped wheels from leaving the running surface. Then wooden flanged wheels appeared which obviated the need for the guiding timbers, since the wheels would stay on the running timbers by the action of the flange.

By the early eighteenth century coal mining was becoming established in Britain, especially in the Tyneside area, and numerous wagonways were built from the mine exits to the river Tyne to carry coal down to the river for onward carriage by sea. In 1787 the invention by John Curr of the L-section iron plate rail completely transformed methods of transport underground. Its successful use in the mines quickly lead to its adoption on the surface for mineral wagon-

An early Tyneside wagonway – the beginning of railways for industrial use. A print from T H Hair's 'Views of the Collieries'.

Richard Trevithick's *Catch as Catch Can* railway on demonstration in Euston Square in 1809. From a Science Museum print.

10

ways in many parts of the country. It was an improvement on the use of iron plates to provide a more durable surface to wooden rails which had first been seen at Coalbrookdale in 1767. The next stage was the realisation that much freer running was gained by using an iron wheel on an iron rail. The consequent loss of friction – and therefore resistance – between wheel and rail meant that considerably heavier loads could be carried in a wagon and a horse was able to haul more than one vehicle. The addition of a metal flange to the wheel proved so successful that the metal flanged wheel superseded all other designs for the transportation of rolling stock over the iron rails. With the use of modern steel (and with the exception of localised urban trains with rubber tyres running on a concrete way as in Paris and elsewhere) it remains the standard railway principle throughout the world.

The harnessing of steam power was first allied closely to mining, though for the purpose of pumping out water rather than in a transport capacity. Mining was being carried on extensively in several parts of the country by the end of the eighteenth century, with the Cornish metal mines and the collieries of Durham and Northumberland ranking as the most important. In both these areas the mines had for almost a hundred years been taking advantage of steam-powered engines to work the pumps which extracted water from the deep workings. At this time, however, there was insufficient knowledge of the ideal combinations of materials and design techniques to take full advantage of the capabilities of steam and the pressures at which engines would work were seriously limited. The Newcomen engine, the first successful example of which was built to pump water near Dudley Castle in 1712, used steam not as a direct method of propulsion but to create a vacuum against which atmospheric pressure reacted to move a piston. The amount of steam required to produce the vacuum meant that the Newcomen engines were huge. They were also very slow running. James Watt improved the engine by enclosing both ends of the cylinder and making the piston double acting, but it was Richard Trevithick, a Cornishman, who designed a steam engine in which pressure of the steam was directly responsible for moving the piston, at the same time allowing the exhaust to discharge into the atmosphere rather than condense. The harnessing of steam at high pressure thus became possible and much more power could be generated from a cylinder of a given size. Now it became conceivable for a vehicle to be constructed which would propel itself by the use of high pressure steam on a piston head and which would also have sufficient power to haul an additional load. The steam locomotive engine was almost in sight.

After a number of pioneers had tried to build such a machine in the late eighteenth century, Trevithick constructed a road locomotive in 1801 and two years later was closely involved in the design and building of what is now accepted as the first steam locomotive to be tried on rails – at Coalbrookdale ironworks. In 1804 his second steam locomotive hauled a ten-ton load over a distance of 9.5 miles in four hours at Pen-y-Darren Tramway, South Wales. Although the trial, which won a wager of 500 guineas, was successful, it presaged a problem which was to plague many a locomotive builder in the future: the weight of the engine was such that it broke the rails.

Thus it was not long before the 'locomotive' was demoted to function as a stationary engine powering a hammer at the ironworks – the purpose for which it was originally intended. Indeed, none of Trevithick's four locomotives was put to prolonged commercial rail use and even his last engine, built in 1808, which hauled passenger wagons round a small circular track as an entertainment near what is now the University of London at Euston, did not last long. Certainly at that time it did not inspire the imagination of anybody with what the potential of a steam railway might be.

The technical problem of supporting the weight of locomotives was to remain unsolved for several years. The cast-iron rails of the early railways could not sustain the shock imposed by the weight of passing trains for long, even after the introduction of the fish-bellied shape. Somehow the engine designers had to resolve the problem of building locomotives which could carry sufficient weight to gain the necessary grip between their iron wheels and the iron rails but were not so heavy that they damaged the track. Many of the horse-worked tramways and railways had been built along routes which included some fairly steep gradients and these presented additional problems of adhesion to the new steam locomotive. For a long time the designers could not find a solution to this weight-adhesion equation and instead concentrated on other means of providing extra grip between wheels and rail. The inventiveness of John Blenkinsop produced a combination of a rack with running rails which gave the Middleton Railway the first successful colliery locomotive in 1812.

A year later William Hedley demonstrated that it was, after all, possible to gain sufficient adhesion for the successful transmission of power through the carrying wheels. In that year his *Puffing Billy* and

Richard Trevithick's pioneer engine of 1803 hauled a train of 25 tons on the Pen-y-Darren tramway (South Wales) in February 1804. It ran on a flanged plateway. Subsequent locomotives to his design were tried out on the Wylam Wagonway in Northumberland on wooden rails.

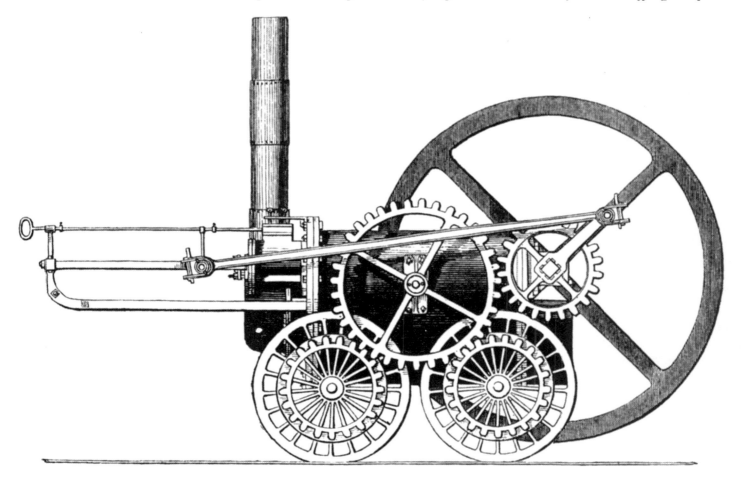

George Stephenson, from the painting by John Lucas.

Early documents relating to the world's first public railway to use steam power, the Stockton & Darlington Railway which opened in 1825.

Wylam Dilly engines were put into service. However, though he had apparently solved the problem of slippage, both Hedley's locomotives were too heavy for the track and to spread the weight they were rebuilt to run on eight instead of four wheels. When stronger rails of wrought or rolled iron had been installed, they were re-converted back to four-wheelers and had a long working life. *Wylam Dilly*, which is now on exhibition at the Royal Scottish Museum in Edinburgh, continued to be used until 1866; *Puffing Billy* is exhibited at the Science Museum in South Kensington, London.

An avid observer of the work of the locomotive pioneers, George Stephenson was soon to emerge with his own ideas. Born in 1781 at Wylam, Newcastle-upon-Tyne, in a cottage beside the tramway, it was not unnatural that he should become involved with railways. This he did by taking employment as an assistant fireman at a local colliery. He became fascinated by the idea of overcoming some of the inherent problems of their operation through improving their design and in his early thirties he was appointed enginewright for a group of collieries in the Killingworth area. Here he was able to develop his own plans for steam locomotives and also to devote time to working out new principles of railway operation and construction.

Like all the early steam locomotive builders, Stephenson faced many design problems with his first engines. He overcame them by some features which gave the machines what would later be regarded as a cumbersome look. One problem to which he turned his attention was the loss of efficiency due to inadvertent condensation. Trevithick's principle of using high-pressure steam relied on there being no condensation either in the cylinder or in a separate condenser. To guard against loss of efficiency the Cornishman had placed the cylin-

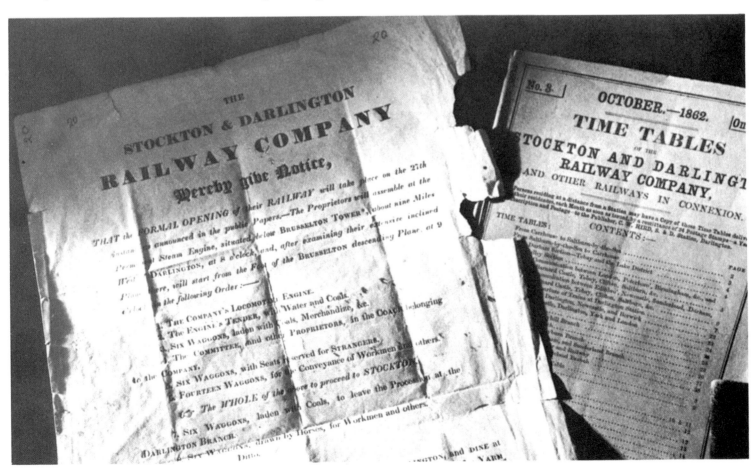

This painting by J E Wigston of Stephenson's *Locomotion* was commissioned by the Northumbria Tourist Board to commemorate the 150th Anniversary of the opening of the Stockton & Darlington Railway.

ders inside the boiler. This, Stephenson also did but rather than siting them at one end, as Trevithick had done, he simplified transmission of thrust to the driving wheels by placing them in the top of the boiler. Cross-beams on the tops of the long piston rods confined the side thrusts during each revolution of the wheels to a relatively small amount and this helped the primitive slide bars or parallel motion arrangements to withstand the force. A basic system of springing cushioned the locomotive to some extent against the shocks which were inevitable from a rough and irregular permanent way and this, by helping to cut out some jumping, improved adhesion between wheels and rails. The springing also had the added benefit of reducing shock and so prevented or at least cut down the number of rail breaks.

As Stephenson developed his work at Killingworth it was only natural that his reputation as a locomotive engineer should spread quickly, particularly as it was becoming obvious that collieries could gain considerable advantages from using their own products to provide the fuel for steam locomotives. Stephenson was asked to build locomotives for other places. Of greater importance at this

The 1975-built full-sized replica of George Stephenson's *Locomotion* was on display at the 150th Anniversary celebrations of the Stockton & Darlington Railway at Shildon.

stage, however, were the plans which he produced for a railway system to provide an outlet for the coal from Hetton Colliery near Sunderland, County Durham. His plans incorporated the use of locomotives or horses on gentle gradients, the employment of the 'falling weight' of loaded wagons descending to pull up empty wagons, or the use of stationary steam engines to haul wagons up inclines by rope. Each of these methods was used when the Hetton Colliery Railway was opened in November 1822. Today one of the original locomotives is preserved at Beamish Open Air Museum as part of the National Collection. In 1925 it had the honour of heading the spectacular procession of locomotives staged to mark the centenary of the Stockton & Darlington Railway.

Opened in 1825, the Stockton & Darlington was also designed to provide an outflow for colliery production, in this case the coal from the Auckland Coalfield which until then had been carried along an inadequate coal road. Proposals for this undertaking, which was even more ambitious than the Hetton Colliery Railway, had first been put forward publicly in 1810 and there had been much debate about the feasibility of the project. George Stephenson met one of the promoters of the scheme, Edward Pease, of Darlington, on the very day that the Act of Parliament granting permission for the railway was passed in 1822. Subsequently Stephenson was appointed engineer of the line and made a number of important changes to the original plans which improved the route and made its future operation considerably easier. It was he who proposed that the company should seek the necessary permission from Parliament for steam locomotives to be used.

Not surprisingly, it was George Stephenson's own 'improved locomotive engine' *Locomotion* which hauled the inaugural train to Stockton on 27 September 1825. It pulled 600 passengers in 38 wagons a distance of 21 miles from Shildon and reached a speed of 15mph. By the end of the following November the success of the new railway had been responsible for bringing down the price of coal in Stockton by one-third; within 18 months it was more than halved and the railway company was already making a profit.

Initially the freight wagons on the Stockton & Darlington were mostly hauled by horses, although it quickly became apparent that, despite their unreliability, locomotives were 30 per cent cheaper to operate.

All passenger traffic was horse-drawn for the first eight years of the railway's existence, this work being sub-let to contractors who used their own vehicles and paid a toll to use the company's line. In fact, the line could be used by anyone who paid the appropriate fee. The Stockton & Darlington Act had specified that the owners of land adjoining the line were entitled to build their own branch lines on their land if they wished. The idea of a public railway with open access and upon which anyone could use their own vehicle proved unfeasible since it was quickly appreciated that there had to be a high degree of discipline and co-ordination which could only be provided under one company. The Stockton & Darlington effectively heralded the arrival of the new style of railway company.

George Stephenson's *Locomotion* and its three sister engines were refined versions of his early colliery locomotive design but they were still unreliable and prone to quite frequent breakdowns. Even so, they compared favourably with the next to be delivered to the Stockton & Darlington, an engine which was nicknamed *Chittaprat* because of the noise it made. This was so prone to failures that it was soon taken out of service. However, its boiler shell was incorporated in the 0–6–0 *Royal George* built by Timothy Hackworth. This locomotive started operating in November 1827 and proved a far more successful machine. It was the first of the double-tender locomotives designed by Hackworth which were to become characteristic of the Stockton & Darlington. Two later engines of this design are preserved: *Samson* in New Glasgow, Nova Scotia, and *Derwent* at Darlington North Road Museum.

News of the success of the Stockton & Darlington spread quickly and it rapidly became an object of close study by many of those who wished to promote or build new railways. Stephenson's fame had spread still more rapidly and even before the S & D was opened he had been approached by the directors of the Liverpool & Manchester Railway. With the approval of the S & D directors, Stephenson

An old Hackworth locomotive at
South Hetton Colliery 10 October
1947.

accepted an offer to become engineer of what was to be an even
bigger project.

The Liverpool & Manchester Railway was the first to be designed
from the outset to incorporate all the ingredients of an inter-city
railway for freight and passengers. Previously, as we have seen, the
first consideration had been the provision of good outlet routes for
mining production. The importance of the L & MR scheme was
that it would connect two major centres of industry and commerce,
both of which were growing rapidly and could only become more
important to the economic strength of the region. The existing,
highly developed water transport system by river and canal was
extremely well used and companies were paying annual dividends
of 50 per cent and more. Railway speculators saw that the time was
ripe for their new transport system to take a share of the profits and
they set about turning the proposals – which had been talked about
for several years – into reality.

When Stephenson took up his new appointment in May of 1824
he immediately put in hand route surveying so that the path of the
necessary Parliamentary formalities could be smoothed by presentation of a route which could be seen to be feasible. In view of the
strength of the water transport industry throughout Lancashire it
was hardly surprising that the L & MR proposals met with considerable opposition from this direction or that water transport rates were
cut by 25 per cent in advance of the railway opening to dissuade
potential customers from switching their allegiance.

By the end of 1824 – before his Stockton & Darlington project
was completed – Stephenson's survey of the L & MR route had been
finished and the Bill was presented before Parliament. Now came a
setback: work on the Bill had obviously been rushed and the opposition was quick to seize any gaps in the information and to have the
Bill thrown out. It was to be another year before the company,
having carried out another, fuller survey, saw the Act passed. In the
meantime a good deal of behind-the-scenes dealing had gone on to
buy off the opposition.

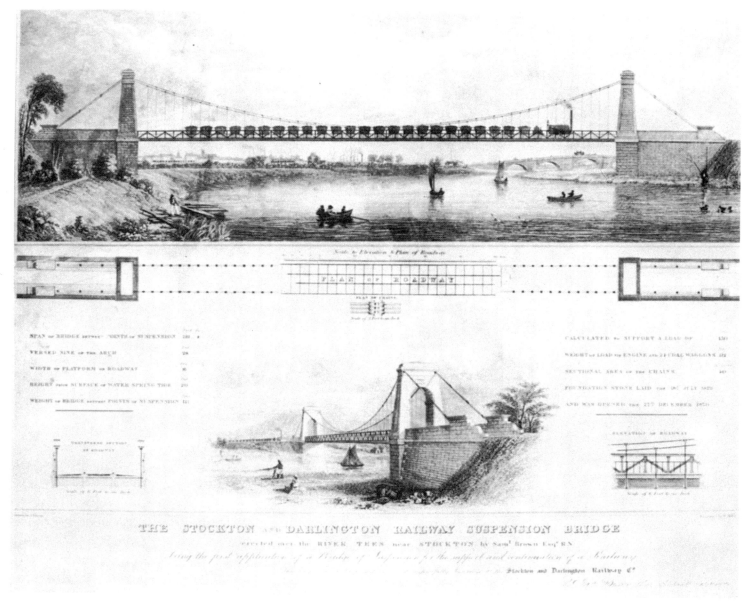

THE STOCKTON AND DARLINGTON RAILWAY SUSPENSION BRIDGE

J Dixon's engraving shows the elevation and plan of the suspension bridge carrying the Stockton & Darlington Railway over the river Tees near Stockton.

The final line of the Liverpool & Manchester was chosen to make it the most economic route possible and rather than make unnecessary detours to avoid obstacles, thousands of labourers were brought in to remove the obstacles themselves. It must be remembered and appreciated that civil engineering was still in the infancy of mechanisation; some of the engineering work carried out on this first inter-city line was breathtaking in its size and daring. A cutting 70ft deep, Olive Mount, was hewn out of solid rock; a superb viaduct of nine arches carried the double track over the Sankey Valley; and the rails were laid across the uneasy surface of Chat Moss.

The directors of the L & MR were determined to find the best locomotive to operate their new line and though many had been built after the opening of the Stockton & Darlington, none of them had proved outstanding and unreliability was still a problem. To seek out the best the directors organised a competition, the famous 'Rainhill Trials', in October 1829. This was not a race and competitors had to observe stringent regulations. Each locomotive had to travel 37.5 miles twice – representing the return trip between Liverpool and Manchester – with an allowance for getting up speed. However the distance was not covered in two straight journeys but by the locomotives' travelling backwards and forwards over the

1.75-mile course on Rainhill level, hauling a load. On the first day about 15,000 sightseers watched the trials and public interest continued unabated throughout the trials.

Stephenson had entered his new *Rocket*, an engine which was a considerable improvement on the earlier *Locomotion*. It was *Rocket* that emerged as the eventual winner of the £500 prize, having shown that it was more than equal to the requirements of the trials. *Rocket*'s leading wheels were rotated by short connecting rods braced to the outside cylinders by simple slide bars, thereby dispensing with the overhead beams of colliery locomotives. This new arrangement provided greatly improved efficiency in the use of the steam which was now produced in a multi-tube boiler fitted with an external firebox surrounded by a water jacket. Exhaust steam was emitted through a blast pipe, providing automatic regulation of the fire draught and, therefore, of the rate of steam generation. Indeed, *Rocket* was the first locomotive to incorporate, albeit in fairly simple form, the principal features necessary to propel a machine by steam successfully and economically.

Rocket was, of course, one of the locomotives chosen to take part in the celebrations which were staged to mark the opening of the Liverpool & Manchester Railway on 15 September 1830. Eight special trains carried dignitaries and the common people from Liverpool to Manchester. The guest of honour was the prime minister, the Duke of Wellington, and it was his train which was in the first recorded fatality involving a passenger train. As it stood at Parkside to take on water, William Huskisson, the Liverpool MP and President of the Board of Trade, left the prime minister's carriage and was crushed between the side of it and the *Rocket*, which was hauling a train on the adjacent track. He was seriously injured and rushed by a train (hauled by *Northumbria* and driven by Stephenson himself) to hospital in Eccles, where he died that night.

The L & MR quickly became a commercial success and outstripped the Stockton & Darlington and other companies by using steam locomotives to haul all its trains. Stockton & Darlington continued to use horses for some freight and the other contractors we have previously mentioned also used horses for passenger operations. The L & MR attracted passenger and freight because of its 'all-steam' image and as a result other transport undertakings suffered; for example, more than half the stagecoaches which had worked between Liverpool and Manchester were off the road within three months. By the end of 1830 the L & MR was able to report a net profit of £14,432 on just three and one-half months' operation. The age of the passenger-carrying steam railway had arrived.

2
THE FIRST MAIN LINES

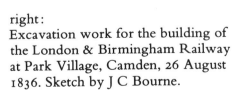

The cutting at Mornington Crescent, 1836, a sketch by J C Bourne of the building of the London & Birmingham Railway.

right:
Excavation work for the building of the London & Birmingham Railway at Park Village, Camden, 26 August 1836. Sketch by J C Bourne.

the development of steamships which allowed Southampton to expand.

Of far greater commercial importance at the time was the city of Bristol, which was still regarded as England's second city in the early 1820s and had a thriving port. The building of the Great Western Railway from Bristol to London was therefore of major significance and the line lived up to expectations. It was superbly planned and executed, with curves and gradients reduced to the minimum by

Grand Junction Railway's Vauxhall station, Birmingham, 1838.

Isambard Kingdom Brunel. It was he, also, who selected the unique gauge for the GWR of 7ft 0¼in, firmly believing that this was the ideal, though it was to present problems later. From the first, though, it set the GWR apart from other companies as doing things differently.

The gauge of the Stockton & Darlington was 4ft 8in. It would be nice to accept the folklore which says that Stephenson chose this after surveying the axle widths of road carts; in fact the gauge was already in use on the wagonways of the north-east. Stephenson saw no reason to change the gauge on which he had carried out some of his early experiments when it was laid on the Killingworth lines. He had used the same gauge on the Hetton Colliery Railway and did so again on the Liverpool & Manchester. It was, of course, to become the standard gauge, though the extra half-inch (to 4ft 8½in) was allowed later to give better clearance between the reverse of the wheel flanges and the check rails. (Today standard gauge is 4ft 8⅜in, the small adjustment having been made to reduce the tendency of bogies to 'hunt' or vibrate laterally at high speeds.)

It was Brunel who introduced the continuous beam timber sleepers for his broad-gauge track. Previously, the iron rails had been laid separately on wooden or stone blocks in parallel rows, with stone blocks supporting the ends of each length of rail. While there were advantages to Brunel's 'baulk road' – the beams gave continuous support and held the track more accurately to its gauge – it also provided a very rough ride since it reduced the vertical give of the rail at a time when there was only a minimum of springing in rolling stock. Despite this, Brunel persisted with the continuous beam until the end of broad gauge, even though other companies had adopted the transverse beam system still followed today. Indeed the greatest advantage of Brunel's 'baulk road' was in the ease with which it could be removed when the GWR finally completed its changeover to standard gauge in May 1892 by converting the track west of Exeter in just two days!

A poster of 1838 outlines the penalties for theft.

Apart from other considerations, the broad gauge created problems because it was incompatible with standard gauge. This meant that when the lines of the GWR met those of other companies there could be no easy sharing arrangement as occurred elsewhere. Such was the extent of concern over the 'battle of the gauges' as it has become known, that Parliament set up a Gauge Commission to investigate each system. When the Commissioners visited Gloucester to witness the transfer of Bristol and Gloucester Railway freight from one system to the other they saw a scene of total chaos and delay. On the other hand, though totally unimpressed with the transfer arrangements, the Commission did come down in favour of the performance of broad-gauge locomotives over those of narrow-gauge. However, that was not enough to stop them from recommending that in future all railways should be built to the standard gauge. Opposition by the GWR to the Gauge Bill made it less restrictive than it might have been and even after it became law, railway companies were able to specify exemption from standard gauge. Broad gauge could still be used for lines built in areas already covered by the GWR. The peak of broad gauge was in the mid-1860s, when 1040 miles of broad and 387 miles of mixed gauge had been laid from London to Weymouth, Penzance, New Milford and Wolverhampton. Even so, inroads had been made by standard gauge into this territory, whose borders were also surrounded by 4ft 8½in tracks.

Brunel was nothing if not an innovator and he adopted an unusual method of propulsion for the South Devon Railway's extensions through the county – the use of the atmospheric system. Though the line was, like other continuations of the broad-gauge system, built by a separate company, the GWR had a considerable financial interest in it, as a major shareholder and as part-owner of the Bristol and Exeter Railway. Brunel was also its engineer.

Atmospheric or pneumatic propulsion had been patented by Clegg and Samuda in 1839 and had been used on the Dublin and Kingstown Railway and also between Croydon and Epsom. The system proposed for South Devon, where it was thought that it would give easier working over the steep gradients around Dartmoor and would cut costs, involved the installation of a 15in diameter pipe between the track. A piston was attached to the leading vehicle through a slot in the top of the pipe, the slot being closed in front of the piston attachment by means of a continuous flexible flap over which a small wheel ran to make a seal behind the piston. It was then possible to exhaust the air from the pipe ahead of the piston by means of stationary pumping engines. Atmospheric pressure entered the pipe behind the piston and forced it through the tube; the train thus was pushed along.

After initial trials in the spring of 1847, the system came into public use between Exeter and Teignmouth in September. Though there were occasional mishaps and delays, the system won universal support and gave a smooth ride and a clean journey. However, complications soon arose, particularly with the leather seal. Not only did it prove to be a popular meal for wayside rats, the leather was porous and was almost permanently saturated or, in winter, frozen stiff. In addition, corrosion set in between the tannin and the fastenings. Less than a year after its public inception, the atmospheric

Early days on the Great Western:
J C Bourne's sketch of the pioneering
days of the 7ft 0¼in gauge:
The engine house at Swindon.

pressure system was useless, the whole of the leather valve from Exeter to Newton Abbot having disintegrated. Faced with repairs which would cost £250,000 and the knowledge that operating costs were higher than had been estimated, the company ceased to use this method of propulsion. The subsequent sale of plant raised a mere £43,000 – a tenth of the capital cost.

Undoubtedly George Stephenson, who had dismissed the method as 'a great humbug', gained some degree of satisfaction from its failure. Nevertheless, Brunel's purpose in decreeing its adoption had been to try a new form of propulsion which could have saved some of the great cost of earthworks and tunnelling involved in trunk-route construction. The fact that the system passed its initial trials was sufficient justification for Brunel to go ahead; the presence of some excessively steep gradients in South Devon are a permanent reminder that in the end he was proved wrong.

Among those who sprang to fame as a result of the new railway age was Thomas Brassey, perhaps the pre-eminent railway contractor, who undertook the building of 1700 route miles in Britain (plus 2800 miles abroad). When Joseph Locke was working on the construction of the London and Southampton Railway, Brassey secured contracts worth £4.3 million to build 118 miles of the line. While working on the Grand Junction Railway, Locke, incidentally, had devised a system of estimating that worked well where a small force of contractors was involved. Brassey's labour force went beyond the 'small' and at one time numbered 45,000 men working in Britain and on the continent. Indeed, British railway builders spread their influence and their labour forces wide: Brassey engineered lines from Paris to Rouen, Le Havre, Nantes and Cherbourg and in Holland and Spain; Brunel surveyed lines between Florence and Pistoia and from Genoa to Alessandria in Italy; Robert Stephenson worked in Belgium, Sweden and Switzerland.

The conditions under which the workmen lived and worked on the new lines were often appalling. Shanty towns were built in the depth of the countryside while, if construction work was being carried out near towns, only the meanest of hovels and most primitive sanitary facilities were provided. The result was that death, disease and injury were commonplace. Opposite York station a burial ground was opened in 1832 for the victims of a cholera epidemic. In the six years required to build the line over the Pennine range more than 100 bodies were taken for burial at Chapel-le-Dale and others were interred near the mouth of Blea Moor Tunnel. Workmen were killed or maimed not only in major disasters such as tunnels collapsing or flooding but also in relatively simple operations. To survive, the men had to be tough and fearless and accidents often occurred when they were showing off their prowess or after drinking orgies which followed fortnightly pay-days. The men were, incidentally, known as 'navvies', a name derived from the 'navigators' who laboured to build Britain's navigable waterways a century before.

Though by no means causing death or disease, the conditions under which second- and third-class passengers travelled were also extremely primitive. They rode in open wagons, some with seats and some without, and had to suffer the smoke and cinders as well as the extremes of the British climate. By contrast, first–class travel was luxurious: passengers rode in covered coaches with a degree of furnishing and upholstery and even oil or candle lights in some coaches. The compartments in a coach derived from the builders' intention to make the carriages as much like a terrace of stage-coaches as possible.

In fact it was possible for road travellers to take to the railways without changing carriages: the road carriages were loaded on to flat railway wagons. This was a sensible marketing idea which proved an added attraction in drawing passengers away from conventional means of road travel. The greatest advantage which the railways had, however, was that they were able to convey passengers more quickly to their destinations.

In 1835 coaching was at its peak with 3300 stage-coaches and 700 mail coaches on the roads each day. However, the Post Office had begun using the railways to transport mail on the Liverpool & Manchester as early as 1830. The introduction of stamps and the penny post by Rowland Hill in 1840 saw the railways poised to carry the flood of mail which was to follow.

When the seal of royal approval was set upon the new form of passenger transport, travel by rail became more than a convenience; it was the correct 'modern' thing to do. In 1839 Prince Albert, who was returning from a visit to Queen Victoria at Windsor, travelled on the GWR from Slough to Paddington. It was three years before the Queen herself was persuaded to journey by rail from Windsor to London but in 1840 Queen Adelaide, widow of William IV, became the first queen to use this mode of transport.

By 1842 far more passengers were using the railways than the stage-coaches. In addition, with a network of nearly 2000 miles of tracks, the railway companies were generating new freight traffic as well as continuing to attract custom away from the waterways. The framework of the main rail trunk system was laid and in operation, the people had taken to steam locomotion for themselves and their goods, and the companies were profitable with an annual revenue of about £4 million.

The curtain was about to be raised on the most dramatic period of railway construction and speculation which would see the trunk send out branches to cover the length and breadth of the country.

Goods shed at Bristol by J C Bourne.

3
THE 'MANIA' YEARS

The high level bridge at Newcastle-upon-Tyne. From *The Illustrated London News*.

The Stockton and Darlington Railway Company's authorised capital when the act allowing its construction was passed in 1821 was just over £100,000 for a route of almost 27 miles, or rather less than £4000 a mile. That act had been the twenty-first passed in Britain since the start of the century to authorise a railway to be built. By the mid-1840s Parliament was coping with a rush of such bills seeking enactment and the cost of railway construction had risen dramatically.

Total authorised capital for the whole country aggregated about £76 million for a route mileage of just over 4000 – or about £19,000 a mile. (In fact by the beginning of 1845 only 2150 miles of line had been opened to traffic.) Yet the tidal wave of new construction against which these figures become mere droplets was still to come. By the spring of the following year there were no less than 519 railway bills awaiting Parliamentary approval, involving a total share capital of around £230 million.

The railway mania had, of course, been set off by the success of some, if not all of the early companies and by the fact that there were still many areas of the country ripe for railway development. The attraction was not generally altruistic; it lay in the chance for personal prestige and fortune for those who could launch successful companies and actually see their railway operating.

Virtually every railway scheme had to have Parliamentary approval and there were various standing orders which had to be observed in an attempt to exclude all but *bona fide* applicants. Because of the queue of bills awaiting approval, attempts were made to shorten the procedure in the House of Commons but even so the presentation of each bill gave its opponents a chance to raise all kinds

Paddington station 1854. From *The Illustrated London News*.

of objections to its contents or the likely consequences if it was passed. In particular, there was opposition from those speaking on behalf of existing railway companies which felt their own interests might be damaged by a new company in opposition.

Even after the Acts had been passed the opposition to new lines did not always stop. Apart from deliberate attempts to prevent the new companies raising the necessary capital, there were also ways of delaying the construction work itself once it got under way. Fights between navvies and gangs of 'roughs' raised by the opposition occurred quite often.

In the 1840s company accountancy was a generally haphazard affair and the companies were required only to account to their shareholders – and even then in broad detail. There was no obligation to present detailed financial accounts to Parliament, the Board of Trade or the public. It was easy enough, anyway, to conceal details of, for example, expenditure from the revenue account by lumping it under the heading of 'capital', thereby apparently increasing the profitability of an operation and, where possible, enabling dividends to be paid out of capital. Railway companies could conceal their shaky foundations well enough to be able to continue attracting shareholders' support and new investment.

Nor was it difficult to rig the stock-market value of shares in the railway companies by forcing prices up or down artificially through bulk buying or selling of shares. There was nothing to prevent

The Royal Albert Bridge, Saltash, joins Devon and Cornwall. Built in 1859 it was considered Brunel's last victory. From *The London Illustrated News*.

dubious characters from floating a new railway company and selling shares in it without any intention of proceeding with the flamboyant plans which had been used to attract buyers' attention. The company could simply be allowed to die or be traded off after the dubious entrepreneurs had creamed off their share of the 'profits', the investors being left with nothing. Today it seems extraordinary that in 1836 four different schemes were put before Parliament for companies to operate between London and Brighton; all were unsuccessful yet in the next Parliamentary session six more schemes were promoted.

An indication of the way in which the 'railway-rush' of the 1840s developed comes from the fact that in 1843 24 Acts were passed to permit new lines to be built; in the successive three Parliamentary sessions thereafter the number of bills presented rose to 37, then 248 and finally to 815. Over 700 of these reached the Private Bills Office, the others failing to be considered for a variety of reasons.

From 1845 to 1847 Parliament sanctioned 8592 route miles in three sessions, yet little more than one-third of that total was actually built; the balance of about 5500 miles was either abandoned or quietly forgotten.

Fortunately, despite the highly suspect nature of many of the railway companies of this period, there were those who saw to it that reputable railway construction continued. Once London was linked with north-west England, the next natural objective became Scotland. The Wigan branch of the Liverpool & Manchester had

The Chepstow tubular suspension bridge and the junction of the Severn and the Wye Rivers, 1852. From *The Illustrated London News*.

33

Kings Cross station train shed 1851.
From *The Illustrated London News*.

been opened in 1832 as a small step further north and in 1838 the Northern Union Railway went beyond Wigan to Preston. Two years later came the opening of the Lancaster & Preston Railway. From Lancaster the road mail coaches for Carlisle, Edinburgh and Glasgow were now timed to connect with the trains. In August of 1840, two months after this development, the Glasgow & South Western Railway opened its first section, which connected the city with Ardrossan. Previously the day mail trains between London and Liverpool had connected with the Liverpool-Ardrossan steamer; now the mail could go all the way by rail.

That year saw other important route developments. Through trains were introduced from London Euston to York, following the London & Birmingham Railway's line to Rugby and then taking the Midland Counties Railway route through Leicester to Derby. From there the route was over North Midland tracks to Altofts Junction. The northward advance was furthered by the opening of the Preston and Wyre Railway's line to the port of Fleetwood, from where the Ardrossan steamer service operated thereafter.

The important step, though, was from Lancaster, over the Westmorland fells to Carlisle. George Stephenson was not entirely happy about a route he had supported across Morecambe Bay from Hest Bank to Kents Bank on an embankment and thence to Ulverston, Millom and Whitehaven. Joseph Locke carried out independent surveys and selected a route almost due north from Lancaster over the 915ft high Shap Fells, preferring to climb the heights rather than tunnel on grounds of cost. The challenge of this long haul was one which was important not only to civil engineers building the line but also to those who had to design the locomotives to traverse it. Today's electrically powered trains from the south barely slacken pace up the last 1-in-75, four-mile climb and even have to reduce power to remain within the 75mph speed limit but to the steam locomotives of the 1840s the climb was a trudge. The line from Lancaster to Oxenholme, near Kendal, was opened in September 1846 and at the same time the Oxenholme to Kendal and Windermere line went into operation. Three months later the Shap section of the Lancaster and Carlisle Railway was opened.

The first continuous rail links between Scotland's two principal cities (Edinburgh and Glasgow) and London were forged by the opening of the Caledonian Railway's Beattock to Carlisle section in September 1847 and the Beattock to Glasgow and Edinburgh in February 1848.

On the East Coast route to Scotland a temporary bridge was opened over the Tyne in October 1848. Robert Stephenson's High Level Bridge at Newcastle-upon-Tyne was completed in 1849 and with the opening of his Royal Border Bridge at Berwick in 1850 the East Coast route was vastly improved. Trains still run to and from Euston via Rugby and thence over the various lines controlled by George Hudson, an entrepreneur from the Midlands, northwards to Berwick.

Hudson, a native of York, was one of the first to exploit the railways in the pursuit of personal power, prestige and fortune. His business life had started with a drapery shop but a legacy of £30,000 enabled him to buy his way into the world of railway finance. A tough individualist, he had the money and soon bought the influence which opened up the corridors of power to him and found him seats on the boards of companies. His toughness made him ideal as a 'trouble-shooter' and soon he was attaining company chairmanships as well as the office of Lord Mayor of York in 1837 and he became a Member of Parliament for Sunderland in 1845. One of his chairmanships was of the York and North Midland which had been formed to link York with the London to Leeds lines at Altofts Junction. Not content with this, Hudson went on to lease the Leeds and Selby Railway in 1840. He thereupon removed most of its passenger services so that travellers were forced to go via Methley and his own York and North Midland.

Having secured control of railway traffic between the West Riding and York and Humberside, Hudson went on to increase his power by promoting schemes to extend the Great North of England from Darlington to Newcastle. He hoped to reach agreement with the Stockton and Darlington for a line-sharing arrangement but failed and so drove his line at right angles through the S & D at Darlington. This strange flat 'junction' of the two lines lasted well into this century.

It was Hudson who secured for the North British Railway the right to build the line from Edinburgh to Berwick. Thereafter, completion of the two Robert Stephenson bridges we have mentioned over the Tweed and Tyne, completed the East Coast link between London and Scotland. Not content with his undoubted power in his native northlands, however, Hudson also gained the

The Royal Border Bridge at Berwick-on-Tweed, designed by Robert Stephenson took a little over three years to build. From *The Illustrated London News*.

support of shareholders of the North Midland (as opposed to the York & North Midland) and they voted him into the chairmanship.

In 1844 he was the prime mover of the amalgamation of the North Midland, the Midland Counties and the Birmingham & Derby Junction into the Midland Railway. All three of these railways met at Derby and NM had been in furious competition with the Midland Counties and the Birmingham & Derby to attract customers for through passage to London. As an example of the fare-cutting, the 38-mile journey from Derby to Hampton-in-Arden cost only one shilling (5p).

Though Hudson's motives can be questioned in a number of his dealings, it has to be admitted that others were to be of considerable benefit to company shareholders. His successful appeals to investors in those three companies to sink their differences was an example of this. It also, of course, gave him rule over routes extending from Bristol and Rugby to Edinburgh! Not for nothing was he known as the Railway King.

However, his reign was nearing its end. The existing rail route from London Euston to York ran mainly over lines which he controlled. Not surprisingly he therefore bitterly opposed proposals for a direct line from London to York. This time, though, he was overruled and the Great Northern Railway gained permission to open a route from Askern, near Doncaster, to London via Retford, Lincoln, Boston and Peterborough. Between Askern and York the company used the tracks of the Lancashire & Yorkshire Railway to Knottingley, where there was a junction with the York & North Midland. The London terminus at Maiden Lane was a temporary one. It served from August 1850 until October 1852, when Kings Cross was brought into use following completion in August of the direct line from Peterborough to Retford. In the interim a detour had been made via Lincoln.

The fact that it was possible for the Great Northern to reach York over one of the lines controlled by Hudson – the York & North Midland – was an indication of his diminishing power. The great railway-rush was slowing and the value of railway shares had fallen. As always in such circumstances, questions were then raised about Hudson's management of the finances of various companies and in 1849 shareholders of the Eastern Counties Railway vocally chastised him. Next it was discovered that the value of shares in his companies had been maintained by paying dividends out of capital. In April Hudson resigned his chairmanship of the Midland Railway and a subsequent committee of inquiry found that the Railway King had 'abused the confidence that was placed in him by wielding the power he obtained to forward his own interest'. Nevertheless, Hudson had made an undoubted contribution to the establishment of a viable railway system and he has a just memorial in Hudson House, British Rail's Eastern Region headquarters in York.

Parliament had always shown a preference for a larger number of companies competing against each other but Hudson's successful amalgamation to form the Midland Railway broke this pattern. The Grand Junction Railway took over the Liverpool & Manchester in 1845 and in the following year the London and North Western Railway was formed by the amalgamation of the Grand Junction, London & Birmingham and the Manchester & Birmingham, opened only four years previously between Manchester and Crewe. (Birmingham was reached over Grand Junction tracks.)

The Grand Junction took with it into the new company – destined to become the largest stock company in the world – some of the sections of the West Coast route to Scotland, north of the Liverpool & Manchester line. In 1859 the Lancaster and Preston Junction and the Lancaster and Carlisle Railways were leased to the LNWR and were vested in that company in 1879.

A similar process of acquisition and amalgamation led to the formation in 1854 of the North Eastern Railway to establish a major company for the East Coast route. The main constituents of the NER were the York, Newcastle & Berwick, the York & North Midland and the Leeds Northern.

Parliament continued to exercise control over the formation of new railway companies, which still required an Act. Though there had been disquiet over the size of the new LNWR it had eventually been granted the necessary Act. However, when the Midland Railway later wanted to amalgamate or 'co-operate' with the LNWR and sought Parliamentary approval in 1869, it was refused. Instead the

Britannia Bridge, built in 1850, was Robert Stephenson's masterpiece of tubular construction linking Anglesey with the mainland. From *The Illustrated London News*.

Midland approached the Great Northern, which agreed that its trains could use Kings Cross as its London terminus, running in on the line from Hitchin. This resulted in proposals for a Midland/ Great Northern merger, but again Parliament opposed the idea, which was dropped.

Even so, acquisition and mergers continued among the small companies to set the pattern for Britain's railway system which was to remain almost unchanged until the 'Grouping' of companies after World War I. Whereas the Industrial Revolution was started in some countries by the emergence of the railways, in Britain it was the railways which accelerated the revolution and fed upon the expanding markets which it had provided for travel and transport of freight.

The railways were quick to see the advantages of cheap return tickets, particularly at holiday periods which had now established a new pattern of movement by the populace to the expanding 'holiday resorts'. Since trains on which cheap fares were obtainable were frequently overcrowded, it was a natural development for firms or organisations to want to reserve complete trains for their members. The pioneer in this new market for the chartered train was Thomas Cook with his special train from Leicester to Loughborough which took a party of about 1000 temperance reformers on an excursion on 5 July 1841. Cheap tickets to the Continent were first offered by the South Eastern Railway in 1848 and Thomas Cook began organising Continental holidays in 1855.

The Great Exhibition at the Crystal Palace in Hyde Park, London in 1851 prompted one of the first large-scale organised movements of passengers by rail. One-million people a month visited the exhibition during the six months it was open and they travelled to London very largely by train from all parts of the country and from the sea ports whence they had arrived from overseas. Excursion fares were available for as little as five shillings (25p) return between Manchester or Leeds and London. For the International Exhibition in Paris in 1867 Cook arranged excursions for working men which cost only 34 shillings (£1.70) for four days.

Having at first treated third-class passengers as little more than cattle, the railways now did all they could to attract the working classes to take advantage of their concessionary fares. In 1844 they had been offended by Gladstone's Act which required them to run what became known as 'Parliamentary trains' with proper seating (wooden benches), protection from the weather and fares of not more than one penny a mile for third-class passengers. By the 1850s the companies realized that the policy of encouraging mass travel by offering cheap fares was paying dividends. In fact by 1880 third-class travel accounted for almost 38 per cent of receipts and a decade later the receipts exceeded those for first- and second-class tickets. Even so, little attempt was made to improve third-class accommodation until the middle of the 1870s when the Midland Railway led the way by introducing padded seats and proper compartments instead of shoulder-high wooden partitions. Even then, it was another 20 years before these improvements became widespread.

The companies attempted not only to attract the custom of the working classes on holiday, they also set about providing services to convey working people to and from their places of employment. The coming of railways to the towns had the effect of prompting many middle class families to move to the outskirts or even into more rural surroundings from where the head of the family would commute by train. The physical act of carving the rail routes into the towns also had another effect: much housing was demolished, particularly in working-class areas, and workmen who had previously lived close to their places of work had also to move further away and travel by train daily. The railway companies offered special cheap-rate workmen's trains which, in turn, encouraged the growth of new suburbs. More than this, the needs of railways themselves also led to the growth of 'railway towns' such as Swindon and Wolverton. The former was a small market town until the Great Western Railway chose it as the site for its locomotive and carriage works. By 1851 92 per cent of Swindon's population were employed in the railway workshops. Wolverton was chosen by the London & Birmingham Railway for its locomotive works because it was approximately mid-way along the line and was close to the Grand Junction Canal. By 1851 85 per cent of the population worked for the railway. Similarly other towns grew because they became railway junctions.

The railways were thus playing an important role in re-shaping the whole life of the country, socially, commercially, and even topographically.

LOST

On the Rail Road between Preston and Birmingham, on Friday, 9th of September,

A LARGE
PORTMANTEAU,

of Black Leather, with a Painted Cover, marked in white letters "G. Puzzi," and on the Portmanteau itself a Brass Plate engraved "G. Puzzi," containing a white leather Portfolio, with Trinkets and Jewellery, and a variety of Papers; also a large quantity of Wearing Apparel and Linen marked with the initials "G. P." Also the amount of 150 New Sovereigns, and a quantity of Silver, the amount not exactly known. Among the Trinkets was a large Gold Seal, marked with a double "P."

Whoever will give information of the above loss to Mr. WALTER, 56, Davies Street, Berkeley Square, London, that will lead to the recovery of the Property—or if Stolen, the conviction of the Offender or Offenders—shall be most handsomely Rewarded.

*Sept*r 15, 1842.   London: Wm. Davy, Printer, Gilbert-st., Oxford-st

An 1842 wall poster from the early London & North Western Railway.

4
QUEST FOR POWER

Despite the twenty-five years of pioneering development between Trevithick's first railway locomotive and the Rainhill trials in 1829, the shape of locomotives and the arrangement of essential components continued very much on a 'hit-or-miss' basis for several years after the trials.

George Stephenson's 'stable' of engines for the Stockton & Darlington which followed the *Rocket* were broadly similar but they did not have its high, steeply inclined cylinders. Instead, the cylinders were lowered and their angle altered so that they lay almost horizontally as it was thought that the original arrangement caused unsteady motion.

The first locomotive on which the cylinders were placed between the frames below the smokebox and forward of the driving wheels rather than behind them was Robert Stephenson's *Planet*. This engine, which had one pair of leading carrying wheels and one pair of driving wheels, was of 2–2–0 configuration whereas *Rocket* was an 0–2–2. It was delivered from the Stephenson works in Newcastle to the Liverpool & Manchester Railway only a month after the company had begun its service in September 1830.

Robert Stephenson achieved the objective of spreading the weight which necessarily went with increased power by using more axles. He did so with his *Patentee* of 1834, which was a 2–2–2 with one driving axle behind two carrying axles. Though the London & Birmingham continued to use 2–2–0s and 0–4–0s until 1845, *Patentee* was to establish a successful basis on which Stephenson and other builders could rely for future developments.

Meanwhile the Great Western Railway, with its 7ft 0¼in broad gauge, was setting a style and standard of construction which was soon to become widespread. Other railways had ordered locomotives from specialist builders almost 'off the shelf', choosing available types which seemed to suit their needs. Daniel Gooch, who had been appointed GWR Locomotive Superintendent in 1837 – just before his twenty-first birthday – was not impressed by the design or performance of some of the locomotives which had been ordered before his arrival. He eventually decided to lay down his own specifications. Among the engines which had been ordered prior to his appointment had been two from the Stephenson works at Newcastle where he had been employed. These 2–2–2s, *North Star* and *Morning Star*, had originally been ordered for the 5ft 6in gauge New Orleans Railway but the contract had been cancelled. They were converted to broad gauge for the GWR in 1837 and provided the young Gooch with his first reliable locomotives. Ten more, all bearing Star names, were bought by the company. Other generally similar 2–2–2s were ordered from different builders and later, engines of the 2–4–0 and 0–6–0 types were ordered for freight working. Some of the early 2–2–2s were converted to 4–2–2 tank engines and used on branch lines for many years.

The first of the engines built to Gooch's specifications to emerge from the GWR works at Swindon was the 2–2–2 *Great Western*, which was later to distinguish itself by running at an average speed of over 55mph on the round trip from Paddington to Exeter via Birstol and averaged 67mph between Paddington and Didcot during the gauge trials to which we have already referred. On a falling

This photograph of the preserved 0–4–2 *Lion* was taken during the filming of the *Titfield Thunderbolt* – a well-known Ealing Studios comedy of the mid-1950s.

gradient of 1-in-100 one 4–2–2 had already attained a speed of 78mph. *Great Western*'s average of 67mph was achieved when the locomotive was hauling a load of 60 tons over a distance of 53 miles. The performance was so spectacular that doubt was later cast on its feasibility. However, analysis of the known facts and technical data showed that a train of this power/weight ratio (around 4½hp/ton) could have achieved such a performance. In 1848 GWR trains were regularly running the 53 miles from London to Didcot in between 48 and 50 minutes. *Great Western*, which came out in 1846, was followed by a few more 2–2–2s but then Gooch switched to a 4–2–2 configuration in 1847 with the Iron Dukes. Though by later standards these might appear to have been comparatively crude locomotives they proved eminently suited to travel at high speeds, hauling light loads along the superbly designed London-Bristol route engineered by Brunel. The Iron Dukes, of which 29 were built, had large boilers and fireboxes, 8ft diameter driving wheels and short piston strokes. With an all-up weight of 53 tons, they continued in production until 1855. By that time the pattern for the higher inter-city rail speeds of this century had been established, thanks to the combination of Gooch's engines and Brunel's broad gauge.

While the speed on the broad gauge was steadily increased, the smaller locomotives on the standard gauge could not match the GWR's performance, despite experiments with a number of designs intended to obtain greater power. There was a great fear that larger and higher boilers would induce engines to overturn if they were used on frames built for the narrower standard gauge. One attempt to lower the centre of gravity by matching a low-slung boiler with large driving wheels was made by Thomas Russell Crampton. He patented a locomotive on which the driving axle and big driving

An early experiment was Lane's 2–2–2 long boiler locomotive of 1849. Note the use of guard irons in front of the leading wheels, the continued use of 'concertina' type buffers and the haycock firebox.

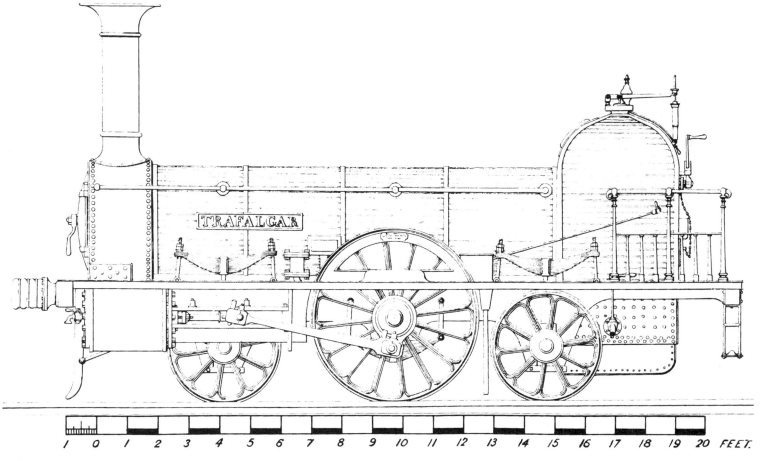

wheels were located *behind* the boiler at the extreme rear, with only small carrying wheels beneath the boiler. Although Crampton's design achieved considerable success on the continent, it was not a high-speed locomotive and though stable it ran hard on the track. However it was a Crampton engine which probably came closest to broad-gauge standards of speed at that time when it ran the 41 miles from Wolverhampton to Coventry in 42 minutes.

Robert Stephenson also brought out a variation in design with his 4–2–0 'long boiler'. It was intended to increase thermal efficiency by making better use of the fuel through the increased heating surface of the longer tubes in the boiler, which also reduced the emission of hot cinders. For operating reasons the wheelbase had to be short. All the wheels were, therefore, placed in front of the firebox. As a result there was an overhang at the rear and this made the engine sway at speeds which would have resulted in considerable wear on the back wheels and could have caused accidents.

The largest wheel diameter ever employed on the standard gauge was the 8ft 6in of *Cornwall*, the famous engine built at Crewe in 1847 by Frances Trevithick, eldest son of Richard, for the LNWR. The boiler was slung below the driving axle, which passed through a channel formed in the top of the boiler. The rear carrying axle ran through the firebox in a transverse tube. In 1858, having put up no exceptional performances, *Cornwall* was rebuilt from a 4–2–2 to a conventional 2–2–2 with the boiler above the driving axle. It now performed better than its original configuration, though no better than other LNWR 2–2–2s with 7ft 6in diameter wheels. *Cornwall* is preserved in the National Railway Museum at York.

The designer for E B Wilson & Company of Leeds, David Joy, came out with a variation on the 2–2–2 which was to lead to future

The celebration to commemorate the centenary of the Liverpool & Manchester Railway in 1938 included the refurbishing and steaming of the *Lion* coupled to three first-class and three third-class replica coaches – a scenario repeated over 40 years later in the spring of 1980 during the RAIL 150 celebrations.

43

development. In 1846 he produced a 2–2–2 for the London, Brighton and South Coast Railway which had a fairly long wheelbase and 6ft diameter driving wheels set outside the frames and carrying wheels inside. This locomotive, named *Jenny Lind* after the contemporary Swedish soprano, had a boiler pressure of 120lb/sq in – unusually high for that period. The name was used for numerous successors and two of these went to the London & North Western Railway. Here they suggested to J E McConnell, the LNWR's Locomotive Superintendent, the idea of carrying *all* the wheels outside the frame. His first 2–2–2s from the company's Wolverton locomotive works came out in 1851 and, like the *Jenny Linds*, had a long wheelbase. All the wheels were outside the frame. The exposed position of the 7ft drivers earned the engines the sobriquet 'Bloomers' (from the contemporary reformer of women's dress whose designs revealed that women had legs!). Further 'Bloomers' were produced with driving wheels of various diameters; they had a boiler pressure of 150lb/sq in and served the LNWR long and well in fast passenger traffic.

In response to a demand by the directors of the LNWR for the company to have locomotives capable of covering the journey from London to Birmingham in two hours, McConnell produced his Patent class of 2–2–2 in the early 1850s. These had 7ft 6in driving wheels and were criticized for their high centre of gravity. In fact their weaker feature proved to be the complicated boiler with a very large fire grate which McConnell intended to burn coal in place of the more expensive coke generally used. Eventually a brick arch and deflector plate were built into the firebox to provide an effective answer to the problem of size. The addition of the arch and downward-sloping deflector inside the firebox door ensured that air entering through the gate or firedoor remained in contact with the fire for as long as possible before reaching the boiler tubes. The arch was first used in 1850. Matthew Kirtley, Mechanical Engineer of the Midland Railway, later began experiments which proved the efficacy of the principle in 1859, after which time the arch and deflector plate became standard features of the steam locomotive's combustion system.

Like David Joy and McConnell, A Sturrock of the Great Northern also adopted high-boiler pressure. He built an experimental 4–2–2 which, though it had 7ft 6in driving wheels, strongly resembled Gooch's broad-gauge single-drivers. It had a boiler pressure of 150lb/sq in but did not put up any exceptional performances.

Another development which later became standard steam locomotion practice took place in the 1840s and involved the variable valve gear to control the distribution of steam to the cylinders. Devised at the Stephensons' works in 1841, it was called Stephenson's link motion. The refinement was an articulated linkage by means of which the travel of the valve could be varied and thus also the proportion of the piston stroke during which steam was admitted to the cylinders. For peak efficiency the admission period needed to be kept short so that steam already in the cylinder when the valve closed continued to work by expanding. In 1849 the Walschaerts valve gear linkage was introduced and remained in common use to the end of steam, its pattern of external rods and cranks easily recognised by enthusiasts.

Daniel Gooch, the Great Western
Railways Chief Mechanical
Engineer and later its Chairman, was
responsible for these handsome
7ft 0¼in gauge 4–2–2 locomotives.

During the first 20 years or so of railways in Britain, development work was not confined to improving the locomotives or to finding stronger, more reliable materials for the track. The railway was a new concept relying on much new technology but it also made use initially of existing transport practices, adapting them as necessary. The builders of the first railway coaches, for example, had a ready-made prototype in the stage or mail carriages of the road. Road coaches usually had four seats inside and bench seats at the front and back of the roof, outside, which took a further ten people. Luggage was held on a rack on the roof while the mail and valuables were carried in a boot on the back.

The greater haulage capability of the steam locomotive meant that more people could be carried and the first railway coaches were built in the form of three or four road-style coaches mounted on a common frame. The broad gauge made it possible to seat eight passengers in a Great Western coach and even the standard gauge coaches were able to take six instead of four people in each section or compartment. Even so, the early carriages were only about six feet wide and they were for first-class passengers only. Some had a box seat for the guard and, like the road coaches, were fitted with rails round the roof so that luggage could be stowed there. To add extra brake power to that of the engine and tender, guards worked the handbrakes fitted to their own coaches.

From 1837 mail was carried by the railways and in 1838 the London & Birmingham Railway introduced a special coach for Post Office traffic with first-class passenger accommodation inside and the mail carried in boxes on the roof. Some coaches incorporated what looked like a projecting 'boot' at one end; rather than for stowing luggage, it was to enable a passenger lying on a paddle board across the seats to stretch his legs. The compartments were only five feet from side to side so that a passenger could not lie down unless there was this extra boot space. A coach of this type was used by the Dowager Queen Adelaide in 1842 and is now preserved in the National Railway Museum.

Second-class passengers who would have travelled on the roofs of road coaches – and could do so on a railway coach up to at least 1840 – were provided with the most basic of accommodation. Though the wagons were roofed they were usually open-sided so that even those passengers lucky enough to have a side wheel next to them still had

A model of a Bristol & Exeter Railway 7ft 0¼in gauge 4–2–2. The engine dates from 1849, was rebuilt in 1866 and became GWR No 2012. The model was made out of cardboard by E G Petrie in 1867.

to suffer the draughts. Third-class passengers were not catered for by some companies and by those who did carry them they were treated little better than animals, riding in open wagons which might, if they were lucky, have bench seats. Holes drilled in the floor prevented accumulations of water in wet weather but that was small comfort to passengers who were probably wet through anyway.

Legislation eventually improved the lot of all, but particularly the third-class passengers. A Select Committee of 1839 inquired into 'the state of communication by railway' and as a result the Regulation of Railway Acts of 1840 and 1842 established rules for the inspection of lines, safety in general and the fixing of fares. The Board of Trade in future included a Railway Department under an Inspector General of Railways. In 1844 Parliament insisted that third-class passengers must be catered for by all companies; the Regulations of Railways Act of that year laid down that at least one train in each direction every day on each line should provide third-class accommodation in closed carriages (roofed and glazed) with seats. The Act, which became known as the 'Cheap Trains Act', also stipulated that trains were to pick up and set down at every station and that their speed must be at least 12mph. The fare was not to exceed one penny per mile. To mark their objection some companies ran the trains at inconvenient times.

By this time second-class coaches had glazed windows and some padding on seats. First-class compartments had plush interiors, padded cushions, partitions and curtains. The third-class accommodation for the 'Parliamentary trains' marked a considerable

Furness Railway's 2–4–0 No 2 of
class E1. These engines were built by
Sharp Stewart & Company in 1870
and subsequently rebuilt as shown
here in 1896.

improvement: coaches were usually four-wheelers, often very well
protected from the weather because there were few windows, had
wooden bench seats but otherwise bare interiors without partitions.

As traffic increased it became necessary to control the movement of
trains. Fortunately, electrical science was developing at the same time
as the railways. Though the electric telegraph was demonstrated
between Euston Station and Camden in 1838 it was not widely used
for some years, either because staff were not literate enough to use it
or because companies could see no financial advantage. Later its
principles were widely used to provide signalmen with a means of
communicating details of train movements. Signalling was rudi-
mentary initially, generally relying on men described as 'policemen'
to give hand signals to drivers indicating whether they must stop,
slow down or proceed at full speed. The railway police were also
responsible for the security of lines and stations.

Mechanical signalling methods gradually took over from hands
and flags. They were usually worked by policemen stationed at
individual signals. One of the earliest and most recognisable as the
forefather of the railway signal (used universally before coloured
lights became common) was introduced on the Liverpool & Manchester Railway in 1834. It was a red-painted swivelling board which
was turned to face the driver of an oncoming train if it had to stop,
and aligned edge-on if the line was clear. Edge-on the board was
barely visible from a distance, thereby complying with the early
principle that absence of a signal indicated a clear track. In time,
however, it was realised that a definite 'clear-track' signal was desir-

able and in 1838 the GWR introduced a swivelling signal with a disc and a crossbar mounted at right angles to each other. Positive danger was indicated by the bar being face on, clear by the disc face on. Since there was still no communication between stations the 'clear' indication was no absolute guarantee of an open line ahead.

With individually controlled signals a train was, at first, allowed to proceed if the policeman judged that sufficient time had elapsed since the last train had gone ahead. In some cases policemen were instructed to stop fast trains and tell the driver how long it had been since the last train had passed. This put the onus on the driver to regulate his speed. Such an imprecise system could be dispensed with when the electric telegraph was introduced. A signalman – the policemen's duties were soon split between men specialising in particular jobs – could ask his colleague along the line whether the previous train had reached or passed the next signalling point and whether the next train could proceed. The line was divided into sections with a signalman at both ends and only one train was allowed on each section at a time. The 'block section' system, as it was called, came into use on some lines in the early 1840s.

The next step from a signalman patrolling the signals and points under his control to operate them individually was to bring the means of operation together in his shelter. The shelter developed into the signalbox and as more levers working signals and points came under the control of one man, methods were devised to guard against conflicting signals being displayed. It was, for example, essential to ensure that if points and signals had been set to clear one route, the levers controlling signals and points on a converging route were locked to danger. Such equipment was first seen in primitive form in the 1840s. In the same decade came the semaphore signal, with an arm held horizontally for danger and inclined down 45 degrees for caution and vertically down for clear.

As main lines were built throughout the country, stations were erected to serve towns and villages along the routes, or even merely close to them. Many country stations had sidings for goods traffic so that freight could be sent to places that, before the railway came, could only be reached by horse-drawn wagon. By the middle of the nineteenth century railways were becoming established as part of everyday life. Long journeys could now be measured in terms of hours rather than days and goods had a countrywide distribution network. In just a few years a way of life that had lasted for centuries had been changed forever.

A 1979-built replica of George Stephenson's famous steam locomotive *Rocket* on show in Hyde Park, London, during August of that year.

An LNWR official postcard of 1904 compares freight trains of 1837 with LNWR's then-modern compound 0–8–0 at work hauling a heavy train over Shap Fell.

Kept to run one of the Director's
saloons on the LNWR, this strange
single wheeler survives today in the
National Collection. No 3020
Cornwall is shown here 'at home'
in Crewe Works.

The London & North Western
Railway 2–4–0 No 790 *Hardwicke* is
now preserved in the National
Railway Museum, York. This
famous engine participated in the
'Race to the North' in 1895.

right:
The Highland Railway around the turn of the century. This painting by J D Goffey shows one of the celebrated *Skye Bogie* 4–4–0s No 85 at Kyle of Lochalsh.

far right:
Midland Railway single wheeler No 118 (now preserved) shows clearly the fine standard of painting with the earlier diamond shaped coat of arms on the splasher.

left:
This Highland Railway Jones Goods
class 4–6–0 No 103 is now preserved.
This engine was returned to service
for a few years in the early 1960s
for special enthusiast excursions.

below:
Oban station in Edwardian days
(from a painting by F Moore) shows
the magnificent livery of the
Caledonian Railway's locomotives.

below:
Virtually all the pre-Grouping railways carried their own crests or coats of arms either on the locomotive and/or coaches. This example was used by the South Eastern & Chatham Railway.

right:
London Brighton and South Coast Railway's 4–4–0 No 64 *Norfolk* heads a Brighton express in the 1911 livery of amber brown. From a painting by F Moore.

left:
A rare example of the Lancashire, Derbyshire & East Coast Railway timetable plus examples of the many ABC types of table available throughout the country.

far left:
This notice advertising the Great Northern Railway Company's hotels would have been affixed to a panel above the seats in first- and second-class coaches to ensure that passengers were fully aware of the services offered. Most of the larger railway companies owned and ran their own hotels.

top left:
A North Eastern Railway class
Atlantic No 726 takes an express to
the north out of York. From a
painting by F Moore.

middle left:
Drummonds T14 class 4–6–0
'Paddle Box', designed for the
London & South Western Railway
in 1911, was so nicknamed because
of its large splashers. No 443 of the

class is shown in this painting by
C Hamilton Ellis heading a
Bournemouth-London (Waterloo)
express passing Beaulieu Road in
1913.

bottom left:
Robert H Whitelegg's massive
4–6–4T of the Glasgow & South
Western Railway heads a Stranraer-
to-Glasgow (St Enoch) boat express
near Ibrox in 1922. By D Goffey.

above:
H A Ivatt's Great Northern Railway
4–4–2 Atlantic No 280 leaves the
south entrance of Hadley Wood
tunnel with an up express during
Edwardian days. From a painting by
F Moore.

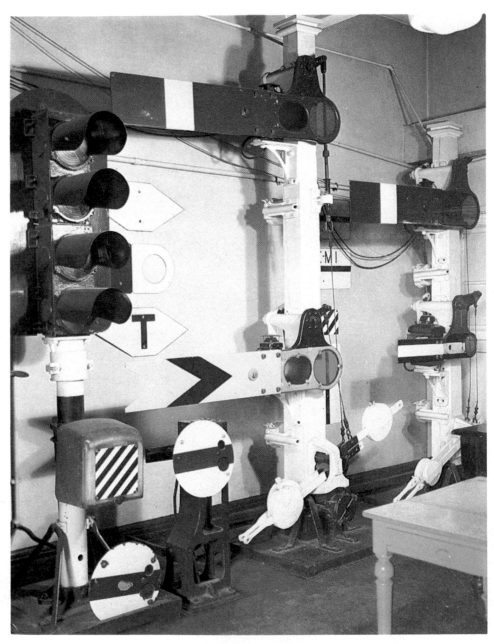

above:
Example of signals as presented at the
British Rail signalling school. On
the left, multi-aspect colour lights;
below, ground or shunting signals;
centre, upper quadrant home and
distant arms; and right, upper
quadrant shunting and *calling on*
signal arms.

left:
An LNER manually operated signal
box on the East Coast main line.
Note the coloured levers, red for
stop signals, yellow for distant signals
and black for points. From the
original painting by Terence Cuneo.

above:
End of an era: Few London & North
Western Railway passenger engines
survived the Stanier and beyond the
1930s but World War II prolonged an
odd lifespan. Here is one of the
Prince of Wales class 4–6–0s to escape
the torch until just after the war –
No 25673 *Lusitania* at New Street
station Birmingham.

left:
Island Railway: The last remaining
steam section on the Isle of Wight
was the line from Ryde to Ventnor.
Since early Southern days most
passenger trains were worked by these
Adams 0–4–4 tanks built for the
London & South Western Railway.
This scene shows a train entering
Ventnor in 1960.

5
RAILWAYS SUPREME

The second half of the nineteenth century was marked by the virtual completion of the British railway map with infilling by more main lines, cross-country routes and branch lines. There were also the development of railway empires, ruthless competition between companies providing rival services over similar routes, and the emergence of strong-willed personalities who led those companies.

The London & North Western Railway rose to a dominant position by further acquisitions after its formation from the amalgamation of the London & Birmingham, the Grand Junction and the Manchester & Birmingham railways. It encouraged and supported acquisitions by other companies if these were thought to be to the LNWR's advantage, and prompted nominally independent companies to keep intruders out of North Western territory. It pressed the Chester & Holyhead Railway to speed up its construction work so that the LNWR could secure the Irish Mail traffic and prevent the GWR from winning the traffic for its own service via Fishguard. The Chester & Holyhead was taken over by the LNWR in 1858.

Euston was regarded by the LNWR as the 'Gateway to the North' and the Great Northern's projected line to London was seen as a threat of serious competition for traffic between London and the North of England. Already in existence was the LNWR's own route from Euston to the Midlands, Yorkshire and the North East by way of Rugby. However, despite LNWR opposition, the Great Northern reached its first London terminus at Maiden Lane in 1850.

Led by its General Manager, Captain Mark Huish, the LNWR also obstructed the Great Western Railway in its bid to extend north-westwards from Banbury to Birmingham, Chester and Merseyside. The Shrewsbury & Chester and Shrewsbury & Birmingham companies fought against the obstruction in alliance with the GWR but the other line involved, that from Birkenhead to Chester, had already become a satellite of the LNWR and in 1850 it was persuaded by devious and underhand means to handle Shrewsbury & Chester traffic. The GWR and the Shrewsbury companies re-

right:
Brunel's 7ft 0¼in gauge for the Great Western Railway ensured steady running at high speeds for the day. Logic ensured that it could not survive as the remainder of Britain's Railway system evolved around the standard, or 4ft 8½in gauge. Here is Bridgend station in South Wales in the later days of the 7ft 0¼in gauge, 1878.

left:
Brighton terminus 1862 – note the ornate station roof, the slotted post signals and the 'birdcage' roof (for the guard's lookout) on the four-wheeled coaches centre left and right.

sponded by obtaining running powers over the Birkenhead line by Act of Parliament in 1851. When, encouraged by the LNWR, the Birkenhead company sought to withdraw from the agreement, Parliament intervened again. At last it was clear that the powerful LNWR alliance could be challenged successfully.

The meandering route of the GWR (the 'Great Way Round', according to cynics) to Exeter via Bristol left a big area further south open to railway development. The London & South Western Railway had extended in 1847 from Bishopstoke (Eastleigh) to Salisbury, which was later to be on its main line to the West Country. In the late 1840s, however, the company planned to serve Exeter via Dorchester and opened the Southampton & Dorchester Railway the same year as the Salisbury branch. The Southampton & Dorchester was planned as a broad-gauge line by local businessmen who had originally intended to lease it to the GWR. However, as the result of a deal between the GWR and LSWR, it went to the latter. In return the LSWR agreed to leave railway development in west Cornwall to the GWR. The London & South Western extended its service to Weymouth from Dorchester in 1857 by obtaining running powers over GWR tracks, while GWR trains continued to serve Dorchester via Swindon and Westbury.

The Great Western Railway's tunnel under the river Severn greatly reduced the distance and therefore the train times to South Wales. Construction of this masterpiece in civil engineering began in 1875 and the work was completed in 1886.

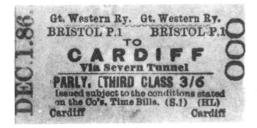

First ticket issued by the Great Western Railway, Bristol to Cardiff via the Severn Tunnel, 1 December 1886.

Last days of Brunel's dream – scene at Teignmouth, south Devon, shows the down 'Cornishman' in May 1892, just prior to final gauge conversion. Note the short sleepers already cut and laid nearby. The locomotive is a small 'convertible' 2–4–0.

The West of England main line from Reading to Exeter via Newbury and Westbury, with a junction for Yeovil and Dorchester at Castle Cary, was formed from a number of minor lines and was not completed until 1906. The route to Exeter opened by the LSWR in July 1860 was from a junction with the Southampton line west of Basingstoke, through Salisbury and Honiton. Overcoming numerous objections and obstructions the LSWR went beyond Exeter north of Dartmoor and down to Plymouth. It opened a through service from London Waterloo to that city in 1876 and completed its penetration of the area with the opening of its line to Padstow on 27 March 1899.

The GWR and LSWR covered individual areas west of Plymouth but for traffic between Plymouth and Exeter and on to London, particularly for Atlantic liners calling at Plymouth, the two companies ran fast overnight trains. Both also developed important holiday traffic, the GWR to resorts west of Exeter and the LSWR to north Cornwall and places on the south Devon coast east of Exeter which were not served by the GWR.

South of London the LSWR competed with the London, Brighton and South Coast Railway for Portsmouth and Isle of Wight traffic. When the first LSWR trains tried to get through in January 1859

Victorian country station: Market Bosworth station (Leicestershire) in 1883 with Midland Railway single-wheeler 2–2–2 No 35 (shedded at Coalville) in the platform. Note the typical small goods yard for local trade and traffic including a cattle dock, coal yard and covered goods shed.

there were fights at Havant. The LBSCR also competed with the South Eastern Railway for traffic on routes along the Kent and Sussex borders.

Sir Edward Watkin, Chairman of the South Eastern at the time, had earlier played a large part in the sale of the Trent Valley Railway in Staffordshire, of which he was Secretary, to the LNWR, the board of which he also joined. In 1853 Watkin became General Manager of the Manchester, Sheffield & Lincolnshire Railway. There he gradually loosened the company's ties with the LNWR and worked up a closer relationship with the Great Northern. He became Chairman of the MS & LR in 1864 and worked vigorously to fulfil his ambition to bring the Sheffield-based company to London. That, however, took nearly 30 years and a long Parliamentary struggle before a Bill for the London extension received the Royal assent in 1893. Meanwhile, Watkin had become Chairman of the South Eastern Railway in 1866 and of the Metropolitan Railway in 1872. He also took an interest in the newly formed Channel Tunnel company. Collectively these wide interests made possible the eventual through-running of trains between Manchester and the Channel ports, via the Metropolitan, the East London and the South Eastern railways, and – given a Channel tunnel – on to the Continent. However, the grand dream of a Manchester-Paris express was not to become reality. Watkin resigned all his chairmanships because of

Derby from the Midland Railway roundhouse in 1860.

A portrait of a guard in full dress on the Cambrian Railways.

ill health only a year after the Manchester, Sheffield & Lincolnshire Railway's extension to London received approval. Watkin's withdrawal brought to an end much of the inter-company squabbling which, while it achieved some worthwhile results, had delayed some important developments.

Even so, while these battles had been going on, extensions of railway service were carried out elsewhere in the British Isles. Cambrian Railways, for example, had a main line crossing Wales from Welshpool to Barmouth and Aberystwyth, and a branch southwards from Moat Lane Junction to Brecon, where it joined the Brecon & Methyr line from over the border. The North Wales coast was served by the LNWR while South and West Wales were GWR territory. There were also various small companies linking the coal mines of the South Wales valleys with the steelworks and ports. As Welsh industry expanded the LNWR made further inroads, serving isolated areas in South Wales reached by jointly worked lines and also obtaining running powers to major centres, even to Swansea, Llandrindod Wells and Llanwrtyd Wells.

The early advance of railways in East Anglia was a slow process, dogged by low traffic and a shortage of capital. Moreover, the first company to turn its attentions north-eastwards from London, the Eastern Counties Railway, caused itself added problems by adopting a track gauge of 5ft. It took some years to realise the error of its

Bletchley station *circa* 1900. A Webb Compound 2–2–2 No 644 *Vesuvius* double-heads a Precedent class 2–4–0 on a long Cambridge train. Unfortunately the identity of neither engine is known.

ways and convert to standard gauge. By the time the ECR reached Colchester in 1843, another company, the Eastern Union, had stepped in and completed a line to Norwich. The ECR was naturally furious and for five years it persistently created difficulties at Colchester, where the two companies' trains connected. In 1854 it took over the EUR. Meanwhile, in 1845, the ECR also reached Norwich over an easier route via Cambridge and Ely. In 1846 it proposed a branch from Ely to Peterborough, intending to establish its own London–York route, but Parliament decided that the Great Northern Railway's scheme should go ahead instead.

The Great Eastern Railway's London terminus, Liverpool Street, which opened in stages between 1874 and 1875, eventually became another starting point for the north as well as for East Anglia. The Great Eastern was created in 1862 by mergers of the East Anglian companies and their various offshoots which ran inland and to coastal towns such as Harwich and Yarmouth. Between 1879 and 1882 the Great Eastern agreed to operate jointly with the Great Northern on a cross-country route from March, near Ely, to Doncaster via Spalding, Sleaford, Lincoln and Gainsborough. When the North Eastern granted the GER running powers north of Doncaster, the Great Eastern was able to establish a through express passenger service from Liverpool Street to York.

In 1876 a third Anglo-Scottish main line was opened, extending the influence of the Midland Railway from South Wales to the Clyde Valley. Despite earlier quarrels the Great Northern allowed the Midland access to Kings Cross via a GNR line from Leicester to Hitchin which had opened in 1857, but the GNR would not allow Midland Railway trains to use the track from Hitchin into Kings Cross at the expense of its own services. The Midland endured the

An LNWR 'Lady of the Lake' class 2–2–2 with a 15-coach train made up of eight-wheeled bogie and six-wheeled stock (about 1900) heads up the West Coast main line. The second and third vehicles carry destination boards.

top right:
Great Eastern Railway up express on Ipswich troughs with rebuilt T19 2–4–0 No 1022 later rebuilt as a 4–4–0 in 1900.

difficulties thus created until 1863, when it gained Parliamentary approval to build a new line from Bedford via St Albans into St Pancras terminus, opened in 1868.

The next Midland Railway goal was Manchester, which presented the challenge of beating the LNWR for London business. In 1867 the Midland opened an extension to Manchester of its Ambergate-Buxton branch. This involved boring the 1¾-mile Dove Holes tunnel through the Peak Forest hills.

The LNWR retaliated against the Midland's invasion of London by extending its influence in Cumbria. Here the Midland's traffic for Carlisle over the Clapham-Ingleton branch of the Settle/Lancaster/Morecambe line had to use the LNWR's main line over Shap. The Midland did not want to build its own route over those fells, which would have been an extremely expensive operation. The LNWR deliberately prolonged difficulties over joint operation between Ingleton and Carlisle and in 1866 the Midland embarked on its own Settle & Carlisle line. This is without doubt the wildest and grandest trunk route in Britain, with long, tough gradients, 19 viaducts and more than three miles of tunnels. After completing this line in 1876 the Midland opened its through service from London to Scotland, operating in conjunction with the Glasgow & South Western to Glasgow, and the North British to Edinburgh.

In the west of Scotland generally the Caledonian and Glasgow & South Western systems intertwined. In some areas they worked harmoniously together but in others less peacefully, particularly on the Clyde coast, where they competed fiercely for traffic. The Caledonian operated the Glasgow, Narrhead and Kilmarnock line jointly with the G&SWR, although the route helped the rival Anglo-Scottish service. A similar partnership covered the exit from Glasgow to Paisley. The two companies also shared a Glasgow terminus at Bridge Street until 1879, when the G&SWR opened St Enoch station and the Caledonian moved to Glasgow Central.

In eastern Scotland the completion of the Forth Bridge in 1890 established the North British Railway as another trunk system. The bridge was made accessible to both Edinburgh and Glasgow traffic by means of a triangular junction built into the inter-city line. North of the river a more direct route from Edinburgh to Perth was opened in 1883 and Kinnaber Junction and Aberdeen were reached with the grant of running powers over the Caledonian's tracks approaching that city.

For about 20 years, from the mid-1840s, Aberdeen had been regarded as the future gateway for railways penetrating the Highlands. In fact the route built north of Perth across the Grampian mountains to Inverness via Forres in 1863 became the Highland Railway in 1865. A line was extended further northwards to Dingwall and Skye in 1870 and the main route opened to Wick and Thurso in 1874. The Skye line was extended to Kyle of Lochalsh in 1897 and in 1898 the Highland Railway opened the direct route from Aviemore to Inverness. Between Aviemore and Blair Atholl the British Rail system reaches its highest main line point at 1484ft on the summit at Druimuachdar.

The Scottish railway system was rounded off by the acquisition in 1870 by the Caledonian of a company which was building north-westward from Callander. Eventually the line twisted and climbed its way to Oban by way of the Pass of Brander after the Caledonian completed construction work, and when the route was opened in July 1880 it attracted considerable tourist traffic. Finally the spectacular West Highland line to Fort William was opened in August 1894, and was extended to Mallaig in 1901.

Railway expansion in the United Kingdom had virtually ceased

Vital bridge: The building of the Forth and Tay bridges considerably shortened the East Coast partners route to Aberdeen. The grandeur of the great cantilevers of the Forth Bridge still appeals today when the smokestains have been weathered away from the approach arches.

The first two return tickets, London to Manchester and back, were issued at the then-new Marylebone station, 15 March 1899.

below:
The final trunk route to be built (and the first to go) was the Manchester, Sheffield & Lincoln's extension south to London (Marylebone via Leicester and Rugby). This picture shows an inaugural train running into Brackley station on the opening day, 9 March 1899. From then on the railway was named the Great Central.

by the beginning of the twentieth century and it was becoming evident that despite Parliamentary controls many areas of the country were already over-endowed with railways. The resulting multiplicity of separately owned stations, depots, yards and competing lines proved a major economic disadvantage, the effects of which have endured to the present day.

Passenger comfort in the closing decade of the Victorian era was one of extreme contrasts. It could still be an austere, trying and wearisome business or a matter of comparative luxury. Passengers were wise to set out with greatcoats and rugs and flasks. They were drawn along in bone-shaking four- or six-wheel carriages which were lit by smelly oil lamps but had no heating. There were no corridors and usually no toilet facilities. Usually journeys were not more than seven or eight hours long – except on Anglo-Scottish runs and those from London to the extreme South West – and these conditions seemed to have been mutely endured. However, an approach to better standards had begun in the 1870s when the Pullman Palace Car Company's superior coaches were introduced in Britain.

George Mortimer Pullman had formed the company in the United States in 1867 to build the higher grade of accommodation required for long-distance trains undertaking journeys of several days. In 1872 the General Manager of the Midland Railway, James Allport, visited the United States and recognised that the Pullmans might be a way of achieving the company's objective of offering better accommodation than its rivals. The Midland had that year taken the contentious step of providing third-class facilities on all its trains. Now a contract was drawn up for 18 Pullman cars to be shipped in parts to England and assembled at the Derby works. Day and night Pullman services were inaugurated between St Pancras and Bradford in 1874. The complete Pullman trains included second-

Midland and Great Northern Railway 4–4–0 No 55 with a train of six-wheeled stock in 1901.

class and third-class accommodation as well as parlour and sleeping cars for first-class passengers. Two years later the Midland's Anglo-Scottish express service included first-class Pullman drawing-room cars for day trains and sleepers on night runs. The Midland had made the astute move of re-classifying second-class travel as third-class and using second-class carriages as thirds. Thereafter all third-class passenger rolling stock was built to what had previously been second-class standards, with padded seats and backs. At a time when other companies were still using rigid wheelbase six-wheeler coaches on expresses, Midland passengers on the Anglo-Scottish service rode in comfort in compartment coaches carried on bogies.

Strangely, it was these compartment coaches which, in the long term proved more popular than the first-class Pullmans with their armchair seating, lamp-lit tables, toilet facilities and centre gangway layout. Even so, the credit for a change of heart by other companies in their design of passenger accommodation must go to the Midland for its introduction of Pullmans and the standard of its own coach-building. Pullman cars were used by a few other com-

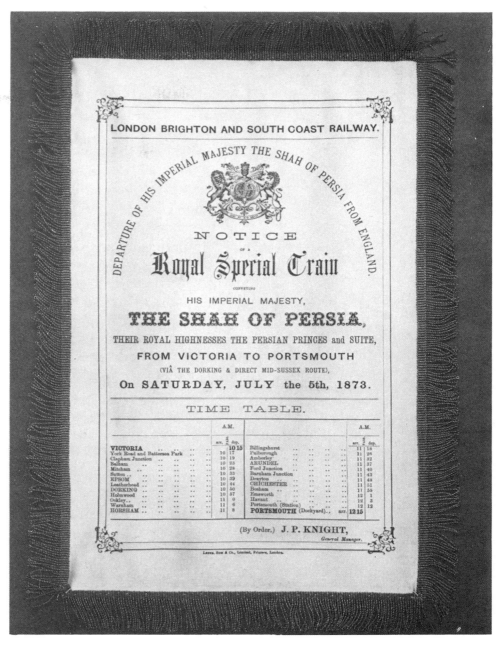

top right:
The cover of the working timetable issued by the London Brighton & South Coast Railway in conjunction with the special train for the Shah of Persia, 5 July 1873.

right:
Alresford station (now on a section of preserved railway) Southern Region British Railways in 1951. This station, once on the Alton to Winchester branch of the London & South Western railway, depicts an example of a one-time numerous but now almost extinct amenity.

panies, including sleepers on the East Coast route and day-time parlour cars on the London–Brighton service. They lasted longest on the short south coast journeys.

The first sleeping cars had been introduced in Britain shortly before Pullmans were imported; the Ashbury Railway Carriage and Iron Company built a six-wheel convertible for use on the East Coast route in 1873 and in the same year the LNWR introduced a sleeping car of its own design on the Euston–Glasgow service. The Pullman retained, for a time, the advantage of having its own built-in hot water heating system. The normal method of heating in lesser passenger coaches was the footwarmer, a type of hot water bottle which passengers hired at various stations. The low-pressure steam method of heating passenger rolling stock was not introduced until 1884 and it was another 20 years before nearly all trains were fitted.

In 1879 a kitchen was built into a Pullman car on the Great Northern. It was demonstrated on a run from London to Peterborough and then used regularly from November of that year for first-class passengers on the Leeds–Kings Cross service. It was the first regular railway dining car with meals cooked on board in Britain. Passengers using the service paid the full Pullman supplement. Although some coaches at this time had corridors there was still no communication between coaches and this restricted the use of a restaurant service. In 1891 the Great Eastern introduced a set of four six-wheeled coaches which had inter-connections. One coach of the set, which

One of Patrick Stirling's 4–2–2 express engines, built for the Great Northern Railway, was used in the famous 'Race to the North' against the West Coast companies. Relegated to more menial tasks in 1901, No 1004 is still spotlessly clean.

was used on the 'North Country Continental' from Harwich, was a first-class dining car while the third-class passengers, who were not admitted to this car, had a folding table on which meals were served from the kitchen in one coach only. It was the GWR which introduced the first non-Pullman corridor train with vestibule connections between the coaches on the London–Birkenhead service in 1892. It did not have restaurant facilities. From 1893 East and West Coast companies introduced complete corridor restaurant-car trains available to all classes.

Despite some tentative experiments with gas lighting, oil lamps predominated into the early 1890s. Lighting by gas produced from oil was tested in an LNWR express in 1875 and first installed widely by the Metropolitan Railway in London in 1876. Experiments with electric lighting were carried out by the London, Brighton & South Coast Railway in 1881, using batteries in a single Pullman and then, in 1889, a dynamo on a four-car Pullman train. The dynamo was belt-driven from the axles and charged the batteries, thus being the forerunner of the standard system employing a dynamo under every coach.

Though the steam train was the fastest means of transport in Victorian years, it was still not as fast as it could have been. Speeds were generally set below those which locomotives were capable of achieving because of the lack of sufficiently powerful brakes, problems of signal spacing, traffic density and the curvature of track – all of

Towards the end of the nineteenth century F W Webb, the Chief Mechanical Engineer to the London & North Western Railway, built several experimental series of compound locomotives using two high- and one low-pressure cylinders. The earlier 2–2–2–0s did not have coupled wheels! These somewhat unsuccessful engines were comparatively short-lived though during their heyday they worked the principle express trains. Shown here is No 519 *Shooting Star* at Chester with a local train around 1900, after being put out to grass by Webb's successor George Whale.

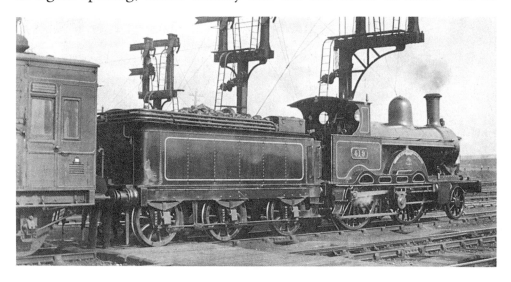

Caledonian Railway 4–4–0 No 729 (later LMS No 14319) of McIntosh Dunalastair I class.

One of William Stroudley's *Gladstone* class 0–4–2 locomotives No 188 *Allen Sarle*. These London Brighton & South Coast Railway engines were kept so clean that it was said that a finger would be unmarked if wiped on the paintwork. The scene is Oxted, Surrey in 1901.

Ex-Highland Railway *Small Ben* class 4–4–0 in early LMS livery (coat of arms on cab side and number on tender – Midland fashion) stands on the turntable to Thurso in May 1928.

below:
A Midland Railways express train makes a water stop at Bedford behind Johnson 4–2–2 No 176 about 1900.

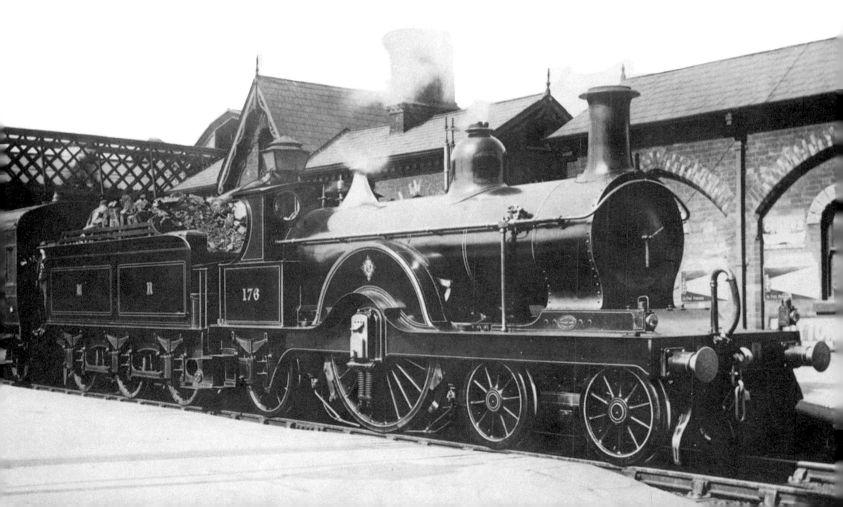

which had to be considered in planning timetables. There were two famous occasions when locomotives were pushed to their limits on the East and West Coast routes. These were in the so-called 'Railway Races' from London to Edinburgh in 1888 and to Aberdeen in 1895.

The announcement by the Great Northern in 1887 that it would admit third-class passengers to its daily morning expresses between London and Scotland which at that time took nine hours to reach Edinburgh was the spur which brought about the first of the races. The West Coast expresses from Euston already took third-class passengers but the journey took ten hours. Accordingly the partners involved in this route replied in the summer of 1888 with the announcement that from 2 June the morning express from Euston would also cover the Edinburgh run in nine hours. A series of leap-frogging moves continued throughout that summer until 13 August, when the East Coast companies scheduled their Kings Cross express to reach Edinburgh in just 7 hours 45 minutes. The first train on this new schedule was late but on the same day the Euston train reached Edinburgh in 7 hours 38 minutes. The East Coast made the run in 7 hours 32 minutes the next day. Such timings were, in fact, impractical for regular operation and thereafter by mutual consent the East Coast set a time of 8 hours 15 minutes and the West Coast 8 hours 30 minutes, the latter's route being $7\frac{3}{4}$ miles longer.

When the Forth Bridge was opened in 1890 it made the route between Kings Cross to Aberdeen 16 miles shorter than that from Euston. The East Coast companies set out to exploit this advantage when the Highlands began to attract an increasing tourist traffic. Thus in the summer of 1895 another 'race' was joined between the two rival partnerships. The two overnight express routes converged at Kinnaber Junction, 38 miles south of Aberdeen and from there the East Coast train ran over the line of the Caledonian, a member of the

Three of these ancient London & South Western Railway Beattie 2–4–0 tanks were kept specially for service over the Wenford bridge mineral branch in Cornwall. Here is the daily goods train at Helland behind No 30585 as late as September 1959.

George Jackson Churchward's four-cylinder 4–6–0 Star class when new in 1910. Note the 3500-gallon tender. The coaches were then in red/brown livery. The locomotive is No 4035 *Queen Charlotte*.

engines on the LNWR were intended to combine the good qualities of single and coupled drive by having two separate (that is, uncoupled) driving axles driven by separate cylinders. On simple-expansion four cylinder engines the results were indifferent but on three-cylinder compound classes, good performance and fuel economy were achieved, though not necessarily only – or even mainly – because of the uncoupled four-wheel drive.

Performance capability of Caledonian Railway passenger locomotives was advanced considerably in 1896 with the introduction of the McIntosh Dunalastair class, which was little more than a standard 4–4–0 design fitted with a bigger boiler. The favourable results with the Dunalastair induced other designers to adopt large boilers. Wilson Wordsell's class R 4–4–0 was in service on the North Eastern just before the turn of the century and the Johnson 4–4–0s with Belpaire boilers of the Midland, and Claud Hamiltons of the Great Eastern appeared early in 1900. The large boiler 4–4–0 was thus set to play a major role at the head of twentieth century expresses.

An even bigger locomotive to replace the Stirling singles was being planned by H A Ivatt. In the United States the 4–4–2 Atlantic type was gaining a good reputation for high-speed running and Ivatt built Britain's first Atlantic-type in 1888. It was No 990 *Henry Oakley*, which is preserved in the National Railway Museum. This, his first 4–4–2 design, had a narrow firebox but he followed with a larger boilered Atlantic design which had a wide firebox more akin to the American originals.

Several railways adopted the Atlantic as the logical successor to the 4–2–2 for passenger express work but as train loads increased, the tendency for the driving wheels to slip on wet rails became a problem. The answer came eventually in the use of three coupled axles on the 4–6–0s and 4–6–2 Pacific types, but they did not become common as heavy passenger express engines until well into the twentieth century.

The steam locomotive had made great progress in the second half of the nineteenth century. The GWR's broad-gauge 4–2–2 of 1847 had been brilliant and well ahead of contemporary design but

The traffic into Waterloo, Charing Cross and Victoria at peak commuting periods has always been extremely dense. Electrification was the obvious answer to quick turnround and rapid acceleration. This picture shows an LBSCR tank with a heavy train of close-coupled stock passing under the Brighton line's overhead electrified wires about 1920 but the train is pure Edwardian.

the standard-gauge Dunalastair of 1896, with much the same size of boiler and grate, could haul trains of twice the weight at comparable speeds.

While trains had become the accepted means of long-distance travel, they also served for short journeys in towns and cities. New suburbs began to be built beyond centuries-old city boundaries and by the mid-Victorian era workers were no longer living within walking distance of their places of employment. Clerks and artisans and workmen moved out from the centres either into the country or to the edge of the towns where they worked. Some railways around London, particularly the North London, Great Eastern and London, Brighton & South Coast, encouraged the resulting commuter traffic with frequent trains and cheap workmen's fares, though the fare levels, as we have seen, were sometimes imposed by Parliament.

By the early 1900s members of the management echelons commuted daily between the Surrey hills or even the South coast and London. A similar pattern emerged around large provincial cities. The Lancashire & Yorkshire Railway, in particular, ran intensive suburban services into Manchester and senior administrators in the shipping and textile industries travelled from as far as the Lake District and the North Wales coast. They sometimes used first-class-only trains which included club saloons admitting members only. Around Glasgow the Caledonian, the Glasgow & South Western and the North British fought for commuter traffic from the Clyde coast dormitory towns.

The in-town suburban trains continued to have non-corridor compartment coaches – often four-wheeled until World War I – hauled by tank engines which were usually small 0–6–0Ts, 0–4–4Ts or 0–4–2Ts. These were supplemented in the first decade of the twentieth century by larger 0–6–2Ts, or 4–4–2Ts or even larger engines on longer-distance services. On these longer-distance commuter trains corridor coaches were introduced earlier as the commuting habit placed people further from their work.

6
EARLY BRITISH LOCOMOTIVES

THE ROCKET
Country of Origin: Great Britain
Railway: Liverpool & Manchester Railway (L&M)
Date: 1827
Length Overall: 6.55m (21ft 6in)
Total Weight: 4,545kg (10,000lb)
Cylinders: 2 203 × 419mm (8 × 16.5in)
Driving Wheels: 1.435m (4ft 8.5in)

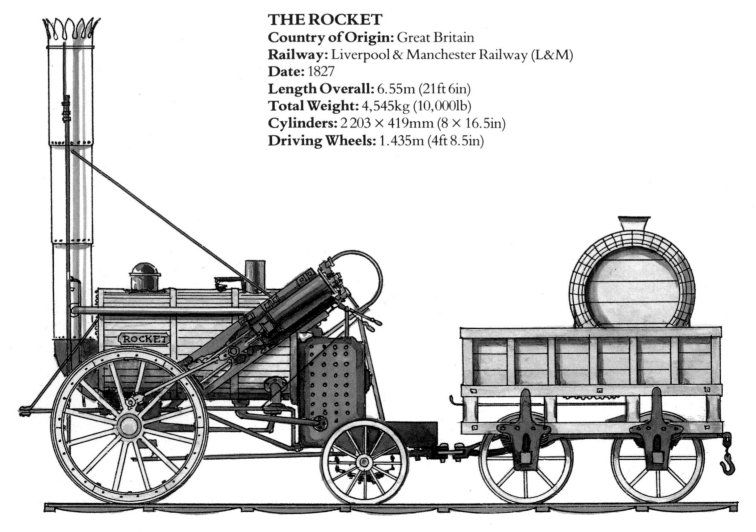

NORTHUMBRIAN 0-2-2

Country of Origin: Great Britain
Railway: Liverpool & Manchester Railway
Date: 1830
Length Overall: 7.315m (24ft)
Total Weight: 11,590kg (25,500lb)
Cylinders: 2 280 × 406mm (11 × 16in)
Driving Wheels: 1.321m (4ft 4in)
Axle Load: 2,955kg (6,500lb)

Fuel: 1,000kg (2,200lb) coke
Grate Area: 0.75m^2 (8sq ft)
Water: 1,817lit (400gal) (480 US gal)
Heating Surface: 38m^2 (412sq ft)
Steam Pressure: 3.5kg/cm^2 (50psi)
Adhesive Weight: 2,955kg (6,500lb)
Tractive Effort: 720kg (1,580lb)

PLANET CLASS 2-2-0

Country of Origin: Great Britain
Railway: Liverpool & Manchester Railway
Date: 1830
Length Overall: 7.42m (24ft 4in)
Total Weight: 13,409kg (29,500lb)
Cylinders: 2 292 × 406mm (11.5 × 16in)
Driving Wheels: 1.575m (5ft 2in)
Axle Load: 5,113kg (11,250lb)
Fuel: 1,000kg (2,200lb) coke
Grate Area: 0.67m^2 (7.2sq ft)
Water: 1,817lit (400gal) (480 US gal)
Heating Surface: 38m^2 (407sq ft)
Steam Pressure: 3.5kg/cm^2 (50psi)
Adhesive Weight: 5,113kg (11,250lb)
Tractive Effort: 660kg (1,450lb)

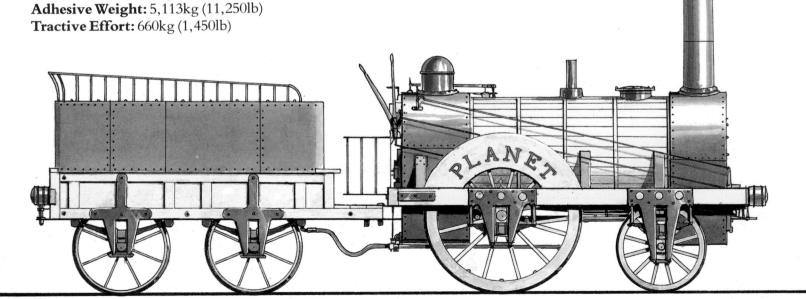

BURY 2-2-0
Country of Origin: Great Britain
Railway: London & Birmingham Railway (L&B)
Date: 1837
Length Overall: 8.168m (26ft 9.5in)
Total Weight: 10,000kg (22,000lb)
Cylinders: 2 280 × 415mm (11 × 16.5in)
Driving Wheels: 1.546m (5ft 0.75in)
Axle Load: 5,727kg (12,600lb)
Fuel: 1,000kg (2,200lb) coke
Grate Area: 0.65m² (7sq ft)
Water: 1,817lit (400gal) (480 US gal)
Heating Surface: 33.2m² (357sq ft)
Steam Pressure: 3.5kg/cm² (50psi)
Adhesive Weight: 5,727kg (12,600lb)
Tractive Effort: 629kg (1,386lb)

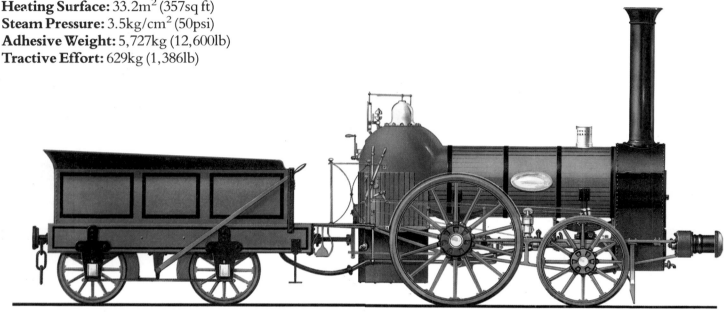

LION 0-4-2
Country of Origin: Great Britain
Railway: Liverpool & Manchester Railway
Date: 1838
Length Overall: 10.287m (33ft 9in)
Cylinders: 2 305 × 457mm (12 × 18in)
Driving Wheels: 1.524m (5ft)
Steam Pressure: 3.5kg/cm² (50psi)
Tractive Effort: 833kg (1,836lb)

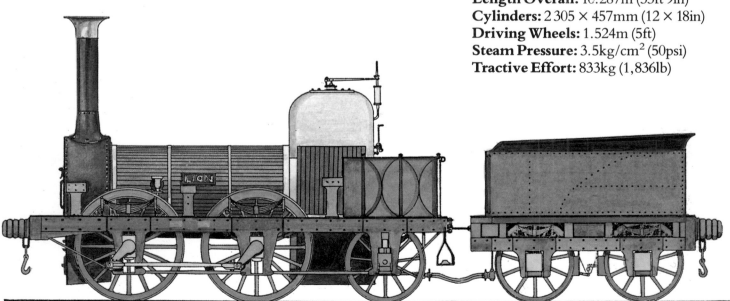

FIRE FLY CLASS 2-2-2

Country of Origin: Great Britain
Railway: Great Western Railway (GWR)
Date: 1840
Length Overall: 12m (39ft 4in)
Total Weight: 42,045kg (92,500lb)
Cylinders: 2 381 × 457mm (15 × 18in)
Driving Wheels: 2.134m (7ft)
Axle Load: 11,363kg (25,000lb)
Fuel: 1,545kg (3,400lb) coke
Grate Area: 1.25m^2 (13.5sq ft)
Water: 8,280lit (1,800gal) (2,160 US gal)
Heating Surface: 65m^2 (700sq ft)
Steam Pressure: 3.5kg/cm^2 (50psi)
Adhesive Weight: 11,363kg (25,000lb)
Tractive Effort: 929kg (2,049lb)

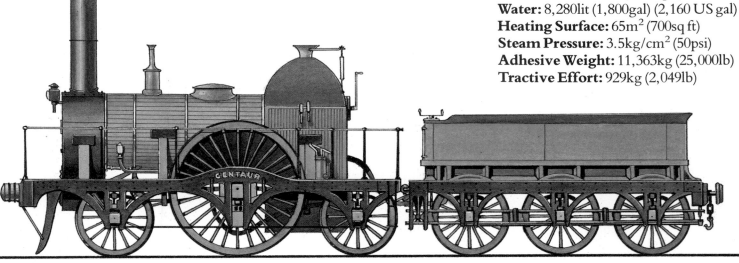

PEARSON 9FT SINGLE CLASS 4-2-4

Country of Origin: Great Britain
Railway: Bristol & Exeter Railway (B&ER)
Date: 1854
Length Overall: 9.372m (30ft 9in)
Total Weight: 50,909kg (112,000lb)
Cylinders: 2 457 × 610mm (18 × 24in)
Driving Wheels: 2.743m (8ft 10in)
Axle Load: 18,863kg (41,500lb)
Fuel: 2,036kg (4,480lb)
Grate Area: 2.15m^2 (23sq ft)
Water: 6,592lit (1,430gal) (1,720 US gal)
Heating Surface: 114.8m^2 (1,235sq ft)
Steam Pressure: 8.4kg/cm^2 (120psi)
Adhesive Weight: 18,863kg (41,500lb)
Tractive Effort: 3,330kg (7,344lb)

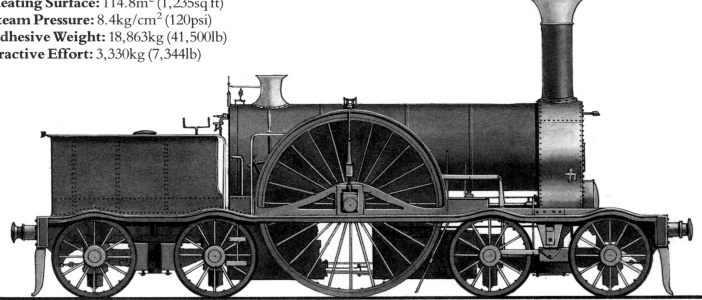

STIRLING 8FT SINGLE CLASS 4-2-2

Country of Origin: Great Britain
Railway: Great Northern Railway (GNR)
Date: 1870
Length Overall: 15.24m (50ft 2in)
Total Weight: 66,136kg (145,500lb)
Cylinders: 2 457 × 711mm (18 × 28in)
Driving Wheels: 2.463m (8ft 1in)
Axle Load: 15,454kg (34,000lb)
Fuel: 3,409kg (7,500lb)
Grate Area: 1.64m² (17.65sq ft)
Water: 13,369lit (2,900gal) (3,480 US gal)
Heating Surface: 108m² (1,165sq ft)
Steam Pressure: 9.8kg/cm² (140psi)
Adhesive Weight: 15,727kg (34,600lb)
Tractive Effort: 5,101kg (11,245lb)

DUKE CLASS 4-4-0

Country of Origin: Great Britain
Railway: Highland Railway (HR)
Date: 1874
Length Overall: 15.62m (51ft 3in)
Total Weight: 73,409kg (161,500lb)
Cylinders: 2 457 × 610mm (18 × 24in)
Driving Wheels: 1.92m (6ft 3.5in)
Axle Load: 14,318kg (31,500lb)
Fuel: 4,091kg (9,000lb)
Grate Area: 1.51m² (16.25sq ft)
Water: 8,298lit (1,800gal) (2,160 US gal)
Heating Surface: 114m² (1,228sq ft)
Steam Pressure: 9.84kg/cm² (140psi)
Adhesive Weight: 27,045kg (59,500lb)
Tractive Effort: 5,597kg (12,338lb)

JOHNSON MIDLAND SINGLE 4-2-2

Country of Origin: Great Britain
Railway: Midland Railway (MR)
Date: 1887
Length Overall: 16.038m (52ft 7.5in)
Total Weight: 82,500kg (181,500lb)
Cylinders: 2 483 × 660mm (19 × 26in)
Driving Wheels: 2.375m (7ft 11.5in)
Axle Load: 17,954kg (39,500lb)
Fuel: 4,000kg (8,800lb)
Grate Area: 1.82m² (19.6sq ft)
Water: 15,902lit (3,500gal) (4,200 US gal)
Heating Surface: 115m² (1,237sq ft)
Steam Pressure: 12kg/cm² (170psi)
Adhesive Weight: 17,950kg (39,500lb)
Tractive Effort: 6,582kg (14,506lb)

TEUTONIC CLASS 2-2-2-0

Country of Origin: Great Britain
Railway: London & North Western Railway (LNWR)
Date: 1889
Length Overall: 15.552m (51ft 0.25in)
Total Weight: 71,818kg (158,000lb)
Cylinders: HP:2 356 × 610mm (14 × 24in);
LP:1 762 × 610mm (30 × 24in)
Driving Wheels: 2.159m (7ft 1in)
Axle Load: 15,909kg (35,000lb)
Fuel: 5,000kg (11,000lb)
Grate Area: 1.9m² (20.5sq ft)
Water: 8,172lit (1,800gal) (2,160 US gal)
Heating Surface: 130m² (1,402sq ft)
Steam Pressure: 12.3kg/cm² (175psi)
Adhesive Weight: 31,590kg (69,500lb)

CLASS Q1 4-4-0

Country of Origin: Great Britain
Railway: North Eastern Railway (NER)
Date: 1896
Length Overall: 17.145m (50ft 3in)
Total Weight: 93,636kg (206,000lb)
Cylinders: 2 508 × 660mm (20 × 26in)
Driving Wheels: 2.315m (7ft 7.25in)
Axle Load: 19.091kg (42,000lb)
Fuel: 5,091kg (11,200lb)
Grate Area: 1.93m² (20.75sq ft)
Water: 18,160lit (4,000gal) (4,800 US gal)
Heating Surface: 113m² (1,216sq ft)
Steam Pressure: 12.3kg/cm² (175psi)
Adhesive Weight: 35,000kg (77,000lb)
Tractive Effort: 7,690kg (16,953lb)

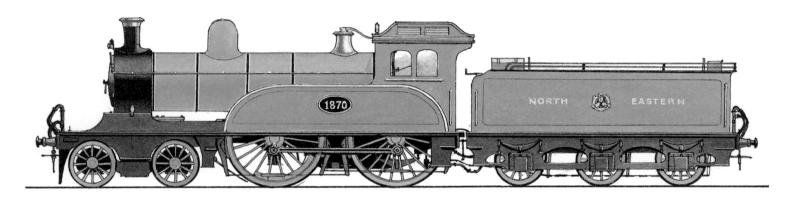

CLAUD HAMILTON CLASS 4-4-0

Country of Origin: Great Britain
Railway: Great Eastern Railway
Date: 1900
Length Overall: 16.276m (53ft 4.75in)
Total Weight: 96,818kg (213,000lb)
Cylinders: 2 483 × 660mm (19 × 26in)
Driving Wheels: 2.134m (7ft)
Axle Load: 18,636kg (41,000lb)
Fuel: 3,246lit (715gal) (860 US gal) oil
Grate Area: 2m² (21.3sq ft)
Water: 15,663lit (3,450gal) (4,150 US gal)
Heating Surface: 151m² (1,631sq ft)
Steam Pressure: 12.7kg/cm² (180psi)
Adhesive Weight: 37,272kg (82,000lb)
Tractive Effort: 7,757kg (17,100lb)

LARGE ATLANTIC CLASS 4-4-2

Country of Origin: Great Britain
Railway: Great Northern Railway
Date: 1902
Length Overall: 17.634m (57ft 10.25in)
Total Weight: 114,772kg (252,500lb)
Cylinders: 2 508 × 610mm (20 × 24in)
Driving Wheels: 2.032m (6ft 8in)
Axle Load: 20,454kg (45,000lb)
Fuel: 65,909kg (145,000lb)
Grate Area: 2.88m^2 (31sq ft)
Water: 15,890lit (3,500gal) (4,200 US gal)
Heating Surface: 182.5m^2 (1,965sq ft)
Superheater: 52.8m^2 (568sq ft)
Steam Pressure: 12.0kg/cm^2 (170psi)
Adhesive Weight: 40,909kg (90,000lb)
Tractive Effort: 7,865kg (17,340lb)

MIDLAND COMPOUND 4-4-0

Country of Origin: Great Britain
Railway: Midland Railway
Date: 1902
Length Overall: 17.26m (56ft 7.5in)
Total Weight: 106,363kg (234,000lb)
Cylinders: HP:1 483 × 660mm (19 × 26in);
LP: 2 533 × 660mm (21 × 26in)
Driving Wheels: 2.134m (7ft)
Axle Load: 20,227kg (44,500lb)
Fuel: 5,682kg (12,500lb)
Grate Area: 2.63m^2 (28.4sq ft)
Water: 15,890lit (3,500gal) (4,200 US gal)
Heating Surface: 122.5m^2 (1,317sq ft)
Superheater: 25.3m^2 (272sq ft)
Steam Pressure: 14.1kg/cm^2 (200 psi)
Adhesive Weight: 40,454kg (89,000lb)

WHEEL NOTATION: STEAM LOCOMOTIVES

Steam locomotives are described by a three-figure combination which refers to the number of wheels, usually made up of driving wheels (shown here as black open circles) and bogie or trailing wheels (shown in blue). The first figure denotes the number of bogie wheels at the front, the second gives the number of driving wheels and the third figure the number of trailing wheels. If the locomotive is a tank engine, a 'T' is added after the third figure.

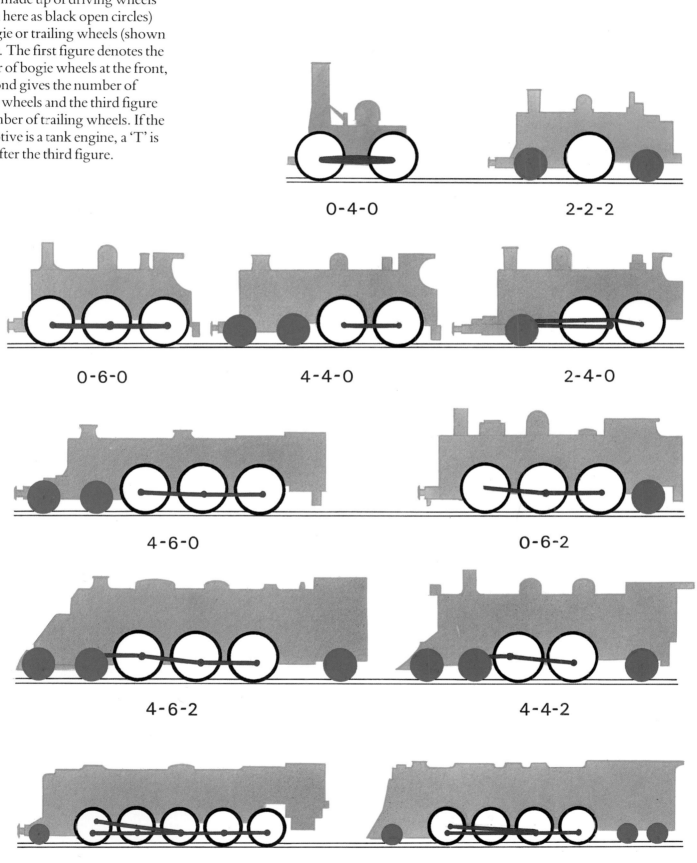

0-4-0

2-2-2

0-6-0

4-4-0

2-4-0

4-6-0

0-6-2

4-6-2

4-4-2

2-10-0

2-8-4

GLOSSARY

Overall length: The length either over the buffers of the engine and tender or over the coupling faces where centre buffers are used

Total Weight: The total weight of engine and tender fully loaded

Cylinders: The number of cylinders is given first, followed by their diameter and stroke. Compound locomotives have both **HP** (high-pressure) and **LP** (low-pressure) cylinders, and details for each are given

Driving Wheels: Sizes given are for the diameter of the wheels as newly fitted

Axle Load: Figures quoted refer to the highest static load as applied to any pair of wheels on the rails. The axle load will vary according to the amount of coal and water in the boiler

Fuel: Unless otherwise stated, the fuel used is coal

Grate Area: The grate is usually formed of cast-iron bars on which the fire burns. The size of grate and thus the size of fire are important as they represent the source of the steam locomotive's power

Water: The amount given is the total amount carried in the tender and/or tanks

Heating Surface: The measure of the size of the boiler comprising the surface area of the fire tubes, the firebox and water tubes in the firebox

Superheater: The area given is that of the superheater elements

Steam Pressure: Intended working steam pressure of the boiler and the pressure at which the valves would be set to open

Adhesive Weight: The weight on the driving wheels of a locomotive on the rails, on which depend the grip between wheels and rail and the pulling power the locomotive can exert

Tractive Effort: This figure represents how hard the locomotive can pull when 85% of maximum boiler pressure is applied to the pistons

List of abbreviations

cm	centimetres
cw	hundredweight
ft	feet
in	inches
gal	gallons
kg	kilograms
kg/cm^2	kilograms per square centimetre
km	kilometre
km/h	kilometres per hour
lb	pounds
lit	litres
m	metres
m^2	square metres
ml	mile
mm	millimetres
mph	miles per hour
psi	pounds per square inch

INDEX